CAUGHT IN THE PATH OF KATRINA

T0289108

THE KATRINA BOOKSHELF

Kai Erikson, Series Editor

In 2005 Hurricane Katrina crashed into the Gulf Coast and precipitated the flooding of New Orleans. It was a towering catastrophe by any standard. Some eighteen hundred persons were killed outright. More than a million were forced to relocate, many for the remainder of their lives. A city of five hundred thousand was nearly emptied of life. The storm stripped away the surface of our social structure and showed us what lies beneath—a grim picture of race, class, and gender in these United States.

It is crucial to get this story straight so that we may learn from it and be ready for that stark inevitability, the next time. When seen through a social science lens, Katrina informs us of the real human costs of a disaster and helps prepare us for the events that we know are lurking just over the horizon. The Katrina Bookshelf is the result of a national effort to bring experts together in a collaborative program of research on the human costs of the disaster. The program was supported by the Ford, Gates, MacArthur, Rockefeller, and Russell Sage Foundations and sponsored by the Social Science Research Council. This is the most comprehensive social science coverage of a disaster to be found anywhere in the literature. It is also a deeply human story.

CAUGHT IN THE PATH OF KATRINA

A SURVEY OF THE HURRICANE'S HUMAN EFFECTS

J. STEVEN PICOU AND KEITH NICHOLLS

FOREWORD BY LEE CLARKE

University of Texas Press

AUSTIN

Requests for permission to reproduce material from this work should be sent to:
Permissions
University of Texas Press
P.O. Box 7819
Austin, TX 78713-7819
utpress.utexas.edu/rp-form

♾ The paper used in this book meets the minimum requirements of
ANSI/NISO Z39.48-1992 (R1997) (Permanence of Paper).

LIBRARY OF CONGRESS CATALOGING-IN-PUBLICATION DATA

Names: Picou, J. Steven, author. | Nicholls, Keith (J. Keith), author. |
Clarke, Lee, writer of supplementary textual content.
Title: Caught in the path of Katrina : a survey of the hurricane's human effects /
J. Steven Picou and Keith Nicholls ; foreword by Lee Clarke.
Other titles: Katrina bookshelf.
Description: First edition. | Austin : University of Texas Press, 2019. |
Series: Katrina bookshelf | Includes bibliographical references and index.
Identifiers: LCCN 2019013804
ISBN 978-1-4773-1972-7 (cloth : alk. paper)
ISBN 978-1-4773-1973-4 (pbk. : alk. paper)
ISBN 978-1-4773-1974-1 (library ebook)
ISBN 978-1-4773-1975-8 (nonlibrary ebook)
Subjects: LCSH: Hurricane Katrina, 2005—Social aspects. | Disaster victims—
Research—Louisiana. | Disaster victims—Research—Mississippi. | Disasters—
Social aspects. | Disasters—Psychological aspects. | Disaster victims—
Mental health. | Disaster relief—Social aspects.
Classification: LCC HV636 2005.L8 P53 2019 | DDC 976/.044—dc23
LC record available at https://lccn.loc.gov/2019013804
doi:10.7560/319727

This book is dedicated to two of the brightest lights in the lives of the authors: Kylee Kubat, granddaughter of Steve Picou, and Claire Kathleen Nicholls, daughter of Keith Nicholls.

CONTENTS

FOREWORD

Disaster coming and going, and coming again.

Katrina came and went without immediately causing great damage, so people in New Orleans and on the Mississippi coast thought they had dodged a bullet. As hurricanes go, everyone had seen much worse. The Storm of the Century ultimately caused over eighteen hundred deaths and at least $125 billion in property damage, making it the most expensive US disaster ever. More significant is that Katrina created mental and physical suffering far beyond the body count. It is the personal sadness and collective trauma that make Katrina so important as a disaster. That's what this book is about.

The assault on New Orleans seemed particularly vicious. It is productively seen as the interaction of multiple social failures and environmental forces. The storm itself wasn't all that strong, at least by the time it got close to New Orleans. The city's flood control system should have easily accommodated the storm, but flood walls collapsed in several ways. Those flood walls were supposed to help *empty* New Orleans of water when big storms came. Instead they served as conduits for wind-driven flooding *into* the city. Much of the place is lower than sea level and is commonly described as a bowl into which the Mississippi River and Lake Pontchartrain could be expected to drain. The city is nearly surrounded by water, and should the worst case come to pass, the bowl could fill, and by doing so ruin property and lives. Worse, once a lot of water arrived, it could stay in the bowl. Indeed it did, and 80 percent of the city flooded.

All of that was predictable before Katrina, so none of the damage and suffering should have been surprising. Yet there we all were, the outsiders, on the afternoon after Katrina came and went, shocked and amazed that the water was *rising* in New Orleans. Apparently, a goodly number of people in and around the city were just as surprised. They had been warned by the National Hurricane Center, the mayor of New Orleans, and, presumably, by most of the people they knew to get out of town. The vast majority did get out, but many did not. Of course, there are always good reasons not to evacuate. It is expensive and troublesome. It means leaving home when threatened by a risk that may or may not materialize. Often, in the United States at least, there are no places for pets and insufficient comforts for children and the elderly, wherever they might go. Besides, experts have been wrong before and might be again. There are always good reasons not to evacuate, which become "foolhardy," "unreasonable," and "irrational" only after an event wreaks havoc on those who bet they will dodge whatever bullet targets them.

A lot of people did not get away with it. Although the death toll was not the highest caused by a hurricane, it was still unacceptably high. There should have been a plan, and that plan should have taken into account poverty, racism, sexism, and all the rest. The plan should have countered all the good reasons to stay put. It did not go unnoticed that many or most of the faces we saw in abject misery after the flood were black. Kanye West put the matter poorly, as he is wont to do, when he haltingly blurted that "George Bush doesn't care about black people." But former mayor Ray Nagin surely put his finger on an essential truth when he referred to New Orleans as a "chocolate city." Two-thirds of the city's population was African American before the storm. Three-quarters of the displaced were African Americans. Most New Orleans residents who have moved in since the storm are Hispanic or white. One could not help but think, "this should not happen in the United States, but I am not surprised it's happening to poor black people."

Caught in the Path of Katrina gives us excruciating detail of the misery. The picture painted by Picou and Nicholls is horrifying, putting great detail on the macroview I just outlined. The chapters are short, adding to their power and poignancy. We know it's going to happen again, to New Orleans and to other places. We saw great damage with Hurricane Sandy, Hurricane Maria, and Hurricane Harvey. It's not a question of whether, as the saying goes, but of when. And when it does happen again, some, perhaps many, people will be outraged, but no social scientist will be surprised. *Caught in the Path of Katrina* gives us a road map for the damage we can expect from future storms. It's only a matter of time.

When the next time comes it will again be the poor and the relatively powerless who suffer most. This assertion is as important as it is obvious. Emphasizing power and position helps to create an accurate analysis of the social system we are trying to understand. If I am correct that the powerful create and maintain those systems, at least to the extent that anyone does, then what we are witnessing in all the pain and trouble after a disaster is the result of relative positions in the social structure. This is not to say that those on the top pull puppet strings so that the powerless are deliberately damaged. Conspiracy theories of that sort are fun to read, but they assert that there is far more control than anyone actually enjoys. It *is* to say that the patterns in suffering are not random. The patterns mean that we are not witnessing some huge operation of chance and caprice. If social stratification is patterned, then so are disastrous assaults on large numbers of people.

Thus are disasters—including creating vulnerabilities, preparing for the "inevitable," and responding to the event we never (always) knew was coming—prosaic. Whether or not we should be frightened as we stare down that beast is confusing. I do not know which is more fear-worthy, the blowing hurricane or the social arrangements that dangle people in its howling fury. Picou and Nicholls tell important data-driven stories about how severe Katrina was, in the winds and the floodwaters. The chapters "Physical Health Effects" and "Mental Health Effects" sound as dull as the papers that appear in sociology journals. But their contents are not dull at all. Our careful chroniclers know the terror firsthand—Picou and Nicholls both live on or near the Gulf of Mexico. "You can imagine my dismay," says Professor Nicholls, "when I awakened in the middle of the night with my ten-year-old daughter sleeping in the next room, while the radio reported the storm was bearing down on us with sustained winds of over 160 miles an hour."

Of course, their knowledge and understanding are broader than personal exposure provides. That's why they could so effectively write *Caught in the Path of Katrina*. Some of the most gripping pages are about what they call "expectations for the future." Such expectations go to the heart of happiness and security, both of which are often reestablished or enhanced after disasters. According to traditional disaster research, these positive outcomes reflect an altruistic community. Such a community is a web of connected people who care for each other, contributing to resilience and recovery.

Such does not always happen. Sometimes a "corrosive community" emerges, and instead of the usual post-disaster feelings of bonding, people split apart. Misery increases rather than abates. Substance and alcohol abuse go up, as do divorce rates. There is a general sense that things aren't going to return to normal, let alone get better. The disorder of disaster becomes the order of the day.

What the authors of this book have seen so clearly is that in disasters whose provenance is defined as anthropogenic, communities do *not* respond in an other-regarding way. Community members do not take care of themselves and others. They do not adjust well to interpretations of what has happened to them or what they expect to happen to them in the future.

Caught in the Path of Katrina is important partly because it is the only book (that I know of) that is deeply based on direct survey research at two points in time. We can trust the conclusions that Picou and Nicholls come to precisely because their evidence disciplines the pathways they follow to those conclusions. Katrina, the storm, happened about fifteen years ago.

Katrina, the demon, continues to haunt its victims. J. Steven Picou and Keith Nicholls tell us what happened to people and what we can expect next time. They tell us how people's notions of the future have changed for the worse. Ultimately, then, *Caught in the Path of Katrina: A Survey of the Hurricane's Human Effects* tells multiple stories about trust and hope. The news is not good.

LEE CLARKE

ACKNOWLEDGMENTS

This book would never have appeared in print if not for Kai Erikson. Kai provided critical leadership in securing support from the Social Science Research Council from funds provided by the Ford, Gates, MacArthur, Rockefeller, and Russell Sage Foundations for supporting a series of books on Hurricane Katrina. Kai has critically reviewed several versions of the manuscript and through his steadfast support and scholarly counsel, we have completed our contribution. In addition, Steve Kroll-Smith and Lori Peek helped to enhance the overall quality of the book by providing comments and direction in the early stages of project development.

From the beginning of the project until final publication, our staff at the University of South Alabama, including Josh Morgan, Beth Daniels, Janel Lowman, and Selena McCord, have provided invaluable assistance in research, interviewing, data analysis, word processing, and proofreading. The technical and editorial guidance provided by Robert Devens, Sarah McGavick, and Lynne Chapman of the University of Texas Press was very helpful in the process of formatting and editing the manuscript. Last, but certainly not least, the continuous encouragement and support provided by Pat Picou has been most beneficial every step of the way.

CAUGHT IN THE PATH OF KATRINA

INTRODUCTION

I heard on Tuesday (August 23) that a tropical depression had formed over the Bahamas. I wasn't too concerned because these weather systems generally take a long time to develop into anything that might threaten us on the Mississippi Gulf Coast. I was taken aback the next morning when our local TV channel reported that the depression had become a tropical storm named Katrina and was rapidly moving toward south Florida. I recall my wife asking, "Is there any chance that this storm will hit us?" I replied, "No way, we have too many things to do this week—and if it does move into the Gulf, it'll likely head north toward the Florida panhandle." So during the rest of the week, we kept to our normal routine of work and school. After sleeping in on Saturday morning, I was shocked to find out that Katrina had crossed Florida and entered the Gulf as a major hurricane headed for the northern Gulf Coast. As the threat to us became more certain, and more frightening, we decided to evacuate. That was a nightmare in itself, what with all the anxiety and expense, and the terrible traffic. After a week with relatives in Arkansas, we returned to find we had no home, no jobs, no school for the kids. Sadly, we also lost many friends and neighbors. Looking back, I still cannot believe how fast Katrina turned our lives upside down.

SURVIVOR FROM THE MISSISSIPPI GULF COAST

In the early morning hours of August 29, 2005, Hurricane Katrina cut a deadly swath through the Mississippi and Louisiana Gulf Coast region. The area of maximum impact consisted of two coastal counties in Mississippi and five southeastern Louisiana parishes.[1] These seven jurisdictions bore the brunt of Katrina's fury, experiencing winds of more than 125 miles per hour and a massive storm surge that reached over twenty feet in height. The

FIGURE 1.1. Hurricane Katrina over the central Gulf of Mexico on Sunday, August 28, 2005, near the time of its peak intensity with winds of 175 mph. National Oceanographic and Atmospheric Administration (NOAA).

storm itself was followed by levee failures that flooded 80 percent of New Orleans. Millions of homes and businesses were damaged or destroyed, and more than eighteen hundred people died. Counting evacuees before, during, and after the storm, estimates are that Katrina displaced at least 1.2 million people, and perhaps as many as 2 million, many of whom never returned to their previous homes.

In the aftermath of Hurricane Katrina, survivors dealt with shortages of affordable housing, job and school disruptions, and severe financial hardships, as well as ongoing physical and mental health problems. In addition, they endured collective trauma associated with rapid and extended displacement of family, friends, neighbors, and coworkers. All of these experiences contributed to the systemic and continuous shredding of the social fabric, ultimately resulting in widespread family dysfunction characterized by substance abuse, domestic violence, divorce, and juvenile delinquency.

Based upon more than three thousand interviews conducted during two surveys of the people affected, this book examines the human effects of Katrina, providing specifics on patterns of damage, morbidity, and social disruption, and exploring issues of family and community recovery. We document extensively the scope of these difficulties, many of which lingered for years after the storm, and some of which have never been resolved.

On Thursday, August 25, 2005, Hurricane Katrina made its first landfall on the southern tip of Florida as a Category 1 storm on the Saffir-Simpson Hurricane Wind Scale,[2] with sustained winds of eighty miles per hour. On its way across Florida, the storm caused some half a billion dollars in damage and killed seven people. By the afternoon of Friday, August 26, Katrina had entered the Gulf of Mexico as a major hurricane. The National Hurricane Center issued a hurricane warning for the northern Gulf Coast from Morgan City, Louisiana, to the Alabama-Florida line. By early Saturday, an east-northeasterly shift in the storm's projected path was accompanied by an increase in wind speed to 115 miles per hour. As its path started to shift toward the Florida panhandle, Katrina began to increase dramatically in size and intensity.

Prior to landfall, meteorologists call a hurricane's shifting and surging target area a "cone of uncertainty," with projections for when and where it will strike being repeatedly revised and updated. As Katrina strengthened, authorities along the northern Gulf Coast were on high alert, encouraging residents to make ready in case the cone of uncertainty should narrow in their direction. However, it is hard to motivate people to prepare fully when forecasts provide only vague and changing probabilities that the storm will come their way. As figure 1.2 shows, just four days before landfall, the cone of uncertainty did not appear very frightening to the ultimate victims of Katrina. The natural tendency is to wait and wonder whether the storm might prove to be "the Big One" or turn out to be a dud. While the uncertainty itself was somewhat stressful, coastal residents were not kept waiting for long.

In the early morning hours of Sunday, August 28, the hurricane exploded into Category 5 status with winds in excess of 160 miles per hour. Later that morning, the storm turned due north as maximum sustained winds increased to 175 miles per hour. Katrina's minimum central pressure dropped to 902 millibars; at the time it was the seventh-lowest such reading on record among hundreds of Atlantic hurricanes. The storm was not only extremely powerful but also exceptionally large, with hurricane force winds extending 125 miles out from the eye and tropical storm force winds measuring more than 450 miles across. On that Sunday morning, residents of eastern Louisiana and western Mississippi awakened to the news that Katrina's course had shifted in their direction and that the cone of uncertainty had narrowed. Fortunately, winds had diminished to Category 4 status, but unfortunately, there was a far more certain projection of Katrina's landfall—the monster storm was headed their way.

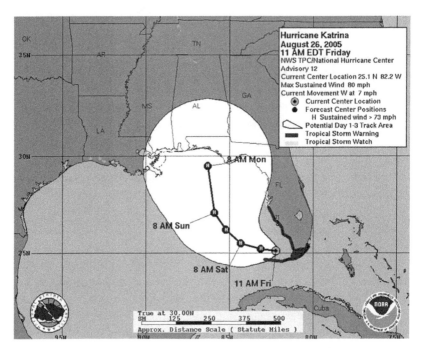

FIGURE 1.2. The National Hurricane Center's Tropical Storm Advisory for Friday, August 26, 2005, just three days before Katrina made landfall on the northern Gulf Coast. The cone of uncertainty extends all the way from southeastern Louisiana to the west coast of Florida. National Hurricane Center, 2005 Tropical Cyclone Advisory Graphics Archive.

Making its second landfall at Buras, Louisiana, Katrina came ashore at 5:10 a.m. central daylight time on Monday, August 29, with maximum sustained winds estimated at 142 miles per hour and a central barometric pressure of 920 millibars. Making its way up the coast at fifteen miles an hour, Katrina pushed a twenty-foot wall of water overtopped with crashing waves, causing extensive damage in southeastern Louisiana. But the storm was far from done. Katrina continued north-northeasterly, churning over the waters of Lake Borgne and making a third landfall at 8 a.m. Monday morning in Hancock County, Mississippi. The northeastern quadrant of a hurricane generally packs the strongest and deadliest punch. Hitting Mississippi with this "right hook," Katrina's winds caused shocking devastation all along the Mississippi Gulf Coast.

Given the storm's diminished intensity from Category 5 status and its track just to the east of New Orleans, news reports in the early days after the storm reported that the large and vulnerable urban center had "dodged a bullet." Regrettably, such was not the case; the bullet was just delayed for twenty-four hours.

Already at risk of flooding due to its many areas below sea level, New Orleans's vulnerability had been dramatically increased by a series of canals that crisscrossed the entire metropolitan area. Although designed to bring economic prosperity, these waterways ultimately brought chaos and ruin. Water flowing through the canals was kept within the banks by a dubious network of levees. As Katrina's storm surge swept through the canals and the levees began to fail, floodwaters poured into the lower Ninth Ward, the upper Ninth Ward, New Orleans East, and virtually all of St. Bernard Parish. About 80 percent of the city eventually was covered with water, which in some areas was more than twenty feet deep. Thus, Hurricane Katrina not only demolished coastal regions with its strong winds and storm surge, but also overwhelmed a major metropolitan area with massive, unprecedented flooding.

SURVEY RESEARCH APPROACH

As tragic and traumatic as it was for those affected, the storm has provided an unfortunately fertile ground for social scientists. Rarely have researchers had the opportunity to study disaster effects and community recovery in such a broad geographical area that suffered such extensive physical damage and widespread social disruption. Hurricane Katrina certainly provided such an opportunity.

In 2008, three years after Katrina made landfall, we conducted a scientific survey[3] of residents in those areas that were most directly and extensively affected by the storm. This target area included two counties in Mississippi (Hancock and Harrison) and five parishes in Louisiana (Jefferson, Orleans, Plaquemines, St. Bernard, and St. Tammany). Our sample consisted of randomly generated telephone numbers using area codes and exchanges for households in those jurisdictions, and including both land lines and cell phones. Within the households, rather than attempting to interview the person who answered the phone, we screened for adult participants (eighteen and older) who had the most recent birthday. These efforts to randomize participation, both in the target area at large and within households, help to ensure that the results of the survey are representative of the full population of the area.

Our survey instrument included 110 questions about actual storm experiences, evacuation behaviors, property damage and economic loss, psychological and physical health consequences, status of recovery, and expectations for the future. We also asked ten questions regarding respondents' demographic characteristics, such as sex, race, education, occupation, etc. The telephone interviews took an average of about seventeen minutes to complete.

Using this approach, we completed 810 interviews in Mississippi in April and May of 2008. In Louisiana, we completed 1,738 interviews from June through August 2008. Thus, we have a grand total of 2,548 completed interviews from this first survey. The basic demographic characteristics of the sample are presented in table 1.1.

In the initial survey, the interviewing processes included gathering contact information from respondents to build a panel for future interviews; a total of 1,352 respondents provided such information. Using these data, we conducted a brief follow-up survey in 2010, completing interviews with 466 of the original respondents between May and August of 2008. Where relevant, we provide findings from the 2010 survey and make comparisons with findings from the initial survey to note changes, or the lack thereof, over the two intervening years.

While there are always questions about the extent to which a survey sample such as ours is representative of the broader population from which it is drawn, we have rigorously followed long-established and consistently validated best practices in the field of survey research. We believe that our approach is the surest way of knowing what the survivors of Katrina were experiencing, thinking, and feeling in the years after the storm, as well as their expectations for the future.

FOCUS ON HUMAN EFFECTS

The most immediate and challenging consequence of Katrina was home loss. Survivors needed a safe place to live, but millions of homes were in various stages of disrepair, and hundreds of thousands were completely uninhabitable. Residents looked to their insurance companies and government officials for help. Unfortunately, the extent of the losses motivated insurance companies to assume a defensive posture in handling claims. In addition, state programs created for distributing funds to help in rebuilding residential and commercial areas have been characterized as insensitive bureaucracies operating with complex and confusing rules and regulations. For years after the storm, completing required paperwork, replacing lost information, filing insurance claims and grant applications, having claims denied and applications rejected, and subsequently filing appeals all contributed to the hardships and extended the burdens on families who were already traumatized by their initial storm experiences. The demanding and

TABLE 1.1. 2008 Katrina survey:
Basic demographics of the sample

		Frequency	Percent
County of residence	Hancock County, MS	160	6.3%
	Harrison County, MS	646	25.3
	Jefferson Parish, LA	664	26.1
	Orleans Parish, LA	645	25.3
	Plaquemines Parish, LA	54	2.1
	St. Bernard Parish, LA	95	3.7
	St. Tammany Parish, LA	280	11.0
	Missing	4	0.2
	Total	2548	100.0
Sex	Male	1212	47.6
	Female	1336	52.4
	Total	2548	100.0
Race	White	1657	65.0
	African American	514	20.2
	Other	114	4.5
	Refused/No answer	263	10.3
	Total	2548	100.0
Education	High school or less	582	22.9
	Some college	716	28.1
	College degree	543	21.3
	Advanced degree	342	13.4
	Refused/No answer	365	14.3
	Total	2548	100.0
Employment	Full time	1170	45.9
	Part time	198	7.8
	Not working	850	33.3
	Refused/No answer	330	13.0
	Total	2548	100.0%

agonizing process of recovery took a toll on vast numbers of survivors, corroding family and community relationships, creating great instability and uncertainty, and resulting in stress, conflict, and the persistence of post-Katrina social disorganization.

Thus, Katrina not only destroyed the built environment but also shattered the social fabric, ripping apart families, social networks, neighbor-hoods, and communities. In many instances, parents, children, and extended kin were separated in the evacuation process and dispersed to distant locations, leading to feelings of isolation and alienation. Having lost homes and jobs, a timely return to the area was not feasible for many of the evacuees. Relocation often involved moving in with relatives, experiencing crowded and uncomfortable living conditions, having no access to transportation, and enrolling reluctant children in new and unfamiliar school systems. Many of these displacements continued for years after the storm, and large numbers of people in these displaced populations never returned to their previous homes. Thus, vibrant neighborhoods were transformed into blighted ghost towns, devoid of their normal work, school, religious, and recreational routines.

For the individuals in its path, the Katrina experience involved substantial physical dangers. In addition to the more than eighteen hundred people killed, thousands more were injured, both during and after the storm. Even those who survived unscathed faced numerous post-disaster dangers, including unstable structures, hazardous materials exposure, carbon monoxide poisoning, electrocution, rat and insect infestations, etc. In New Orleans, the post-storm flooding was disastrous, but the water itself was not the only problem; significant quantities of oil, gasoline, industrial and household chemicals, and other hazardous wastes contaminated the floodwaters. This corrosive toxic sludge contaminated the soil and gave off fumes that fouled the air. For the most part, the effects of the sludge were undetermined and unaddressed, creating the potential for continued exposures and subsequent chronic health risks for survivors, as well as generalized anxiety regarding potential future effects.

Such conditions contributed significantly to declining physical health among survivors. Heart problems, high blood pressure, stomach disorders, rashes, infections, respiratory problems, and a decline in immune system capabilities manifested in both adults and children. The stress and uncertainty associated with these physical health issues resulted in mental and behavioral health problems, including depression, anxiety, anger, and recurrent symptoms of post-traumatic stress disorder (PTSD). Such psychological problems in turn produced and exacerbated physical health disorders in a spiraling cycle of dysfunction. All of this occurred in the context of a general scarcity of health care resources, limited access to health care providers, disruptions in medication and treatment routines, and little or no medical insurance, such that many survivors' health problems went untreated indefinitely. This mental-physical health interactive spiral resulted in a drastic, long-term decline in the quality of life for survivors of Katrina.

OVERALL CONTEXT

To more fully understand the consequences and implications of the Katrina experience, it is important to consider the context in which the storm occurred. Disaster experts view both damage to the built environment and psychosocial effects of disasters in terms of vulnerability and resiliency. These concepts are two sides of the coin of storm-related trauma; they are multidimensional and clearly related to the concepts of hazard and risk.

Vulnerability is the susceptibility to harm or injury that characterizes the human condition at a given point in time, space, and culture. For decades this "tendency to be damaged" has been a topic of extended discussion across disciplines such as geography, demography, sociology, psychology, and meteorology. Greater vulnerability results in greater damage to the built environment and greater suffering and hardship for those who inhabit it, which in turn prolongs recovery and extends the psychosocial trauma indefinitely into the future. This is especially the case when vulnerabilities include not only geographical and meteorological factors, but also economic instability and health-related fragility.

Begun in 1837, archival records of hurricane activity provide compelling evidence of the vulnerability of the northern Gulf Coast. Hurricanes make their way into the Gulf of Mexico with great regularity. Indeed, on average, two tropical storms and one hurricane have struck the region every three years since 1851, for a total of over 500 hurricanes and tropical storms in the last 170 years. Thus, Katrina's impact area was an extremely vulnerable geographic target, with the historically eroding Louisiana coastline and the shallow waters of the Mississippi Sound providing additional physical hazards that increased the potential for Katrina's devastation.

Essentially, resiliency is the ability to withstand distress and bounce back from destruction and devastation. A resilient community, for example, will recover, at a minimum, to the conditions prevailing prior to the disaster, and will tend to do so in a timelier fashion than a nonresilient community. Thus, resiliency is a positive response to vulnerability that facilitates a return to "normalcy" or perhaps a transformation to a "new normal" that might even constitute an improvement over pre-disaster conditions.

The capacity to cope with the destruction of the built environment, the psychological and emotional trauma, and the prolonged social mayhem caused by a disaster such as Katrina, as well as to overcome chronic obstacles that emerge in the post-disaster context, is characteristic of resilient communities. This works to enhance community members' ability to withstand and respond to disasters, minimizing the time it takes for them to recover.

The capacity for resiliency is heightened when communities have thriving economies with effective political leadership and community members enjoy good health, easy access to health care resources, and a high quality of life. Additionally, resilience is highest when networks of trusting relationships exist among community members, as such networks act to facilitate effective communication and encourage cooperation. From an infrastructure perspective, resiliency of the built environment is maximized when roads, bridges, levees, sewer systems, water plants, and the electrical grid are built to the highest standards and are well maintained. While a comprehensive review of these issues as they prevailed in the region affected by Katrina is beyond the scope of this book, suffice it to say that the typical community along the northern Gulf Coast tends to fall far short when it comes to most, if not all, of these characteristics. The lack of resiliency prevailing in much of our target area not only contributes to the trauma associated with the storm experience but also significantly extends the time it takes for recovery.

Ostensibly, a reduction of the negative effects of hurricanes would involve the reduction of all dimensions of physical and social vulnerabilities by enhancing all dimensions of physical and social resilience. Because hurricanes are obviously a part of the northern Gulf Coast's meteorological landscape, one might expect that, over time, the physical and social vulnerability of the area would have been reduced and resiliency would have been improved. However, we provide a different testimony for the costliest and second-deadliest[4] storm to ravage the Gulf Coast of the United States.

WHAT IS UNIQUE IN OUR CONTRIBUTION

The amount of research and literature published on Hurricane Katrina is truly massive. A keyword search for "Hurricane Katrina" on EBSCO's Academic Search Complete yields well over fourteen thousand results of scholarly research published in journals, periodicals, reports, and books.[5] One might think it difficult to make a unique contribution given the overwhelming amount of existing research. And yet, when narrowing our search by adding "human effects" and "survey," we find only eleven items, none of which report the results of a general population survey of a broad target area and cover the full range of topics we review here.

When we review these few similar items, we find that in some cases the focus is narrowed to a subsample of the population, such as displaced residents,[6] university students,[7] or senior citizens.[8] In other cases the focus is limited to particulars like mental health effects[9] or sociopolitical consequences of perception regarding Katrina.[10] One interesting study reports a secondary statistical analysis of our 2008 survey data to demonstrate the social consequences of respondents' storm experiences.[11]

We are not claiming here that this brief review offers an exhaustive elaboration of survey research on the human effects of Hurricane Katrina. We do feel, however, that it provides an illustrative example of the limited amount of similar research and demonstrates that the breadth and depth of coverage in this work is exceptional and almost certainly unique.

In addition to the wide-ranging coverage, we also offer considerably more context for our findings than is typical for those few other academic works reporting survey results. When it comes to the hurricane experience, for example, we review the issues associated with the calls to evacuate, the problems experienced by those leaving the city, the obstacles that prevented so many people from evacuating, and the nightmares endured by those who were left behind. We also help the reader more fully understand the post-storm trauma by providing an extensive summary of the dangers faced by those returning to their homes. These dangers included the destruction of not only their own homes but also the infrastructure of their neighborhoods and the larger community, as well as the toxic contamination that threatened survivors' health and well-being. In the recovery phase, we describe in detail the terms and conditions associated with homeowners' insurance, flood insurance, and state programs to support residential rebuilding. We also provide similar background information for the social, physical, and mental health consequences associated with the storm experience.

Another unique aspect of this work involves our presentation of a series of practical lessons learned from our research on the human effects of Katrina. In most academic literature, research findings are much more likely to validate or invalidate conceptual and theoretical expectations than to have applied policy implications. In this work, however, we address directly the governmental shortcomings and failures manifested in the aftermath of Katrina and offer recommendations for mitigating the negative effects of future storms.

It should also be noted that the findings evident in our survey research on the human effects of Katrina complement the work of disaster researchers in many other fields, such as economics, climatology, and engineering. Studying the human effects of disasters without gaining the perspectives of those who were affected would be fragmentary and deficient at best. The findings reported here, then, tend to balance and give dimension to our understanding of disasters writ large. Our findings also tend to confirm conditions, experiences, and perceptions that have been generally and anecdotally reported in the news media. In sum, we believe that this work will provide readers with new and extensive evidence-based insights into the devastation and disruptions caused by Hurricane Katrina.

GENERAL ORGANIZATION

In the following chapters, we present the results of our surveys with emphasis on the most serious and consequential human effects of Hurricane Katrina. In sum, these results paint a picture of limited regional recovery slowed by chronic financial, social, psychological, and physical health issues that continued to plague residents for years after the storm. The results also reveal a degree of pessimism and skepticism regarding the potential for full recovery as survivors attempted to move forward with their lives.

Chapter 2 deals primarily with respondents' storm experiences and post-storm conditions, including issues of evacuation versus sheltering in place, and details of family safety, separation, and displacement, as well as residential damage, financial loss, and economic hardships. In chapter 3 we review outcomes associated with returning home and family reunification, and provide details on housing conditions with assessments of pre- and post-storm accommodations, including the infamous FEMA trailers. Obstacles to rebuilding are the focus of chapter 4, with information on the processes and outcomes of homeowners' insurance claims and state-administered grant programs for residential reconstruction. Chapter 5 deals with physical health effects, including heart, hypertension, headache, respiratory, and digestive problems, while chapter 6 covers mental and behavioral health effects with a primary focus on symptoms of depression and post-traumatic stress disorder. We begin chapter 7 with a review of respondents' self-reported status of recovery and their expectations for the future, followed by a brief summary of our survey findings. We conclude with a section on the overarching implications of lessons learned from our study of the "Storm of the Century."[12]

EXPERIENCING KATRINA

*My wife screamed, "Where are we going to go?" Governor Blanco
had just declared a state of emergency for south Louisiana and New
Orleans as Katrina was getting bigger and stronger. I responded,
"I hope we're not going anywhere. I bet you it goes to Florida. All these
hurricanes hit Florida. I'll get stuff ready just in case we have to leave,
but it's not coming here!" When Katrina's winds hit 125 miles per
hour at 3:00 a.m. on Sunday morning, I woke her, "We gotta get out
of the Ninth Ward" (New Orleans). I told her to call her parents so
we could pick them up on our way out. I also called my brother and
told him to get out too. He said he was going to wait until later in the
morning to make up his mind. After talking to her parents, my wife
told me her mother wanted to go, but her father was staying, "Daddy
said he rode out Camille, so he can ride out this storm. Mama
thinks he is crazy." We stuffed pictures, keepsakes, and valuables in
the car while keeping an eye on the Weather Channel. At 9:30 that
morning, Mayor Nagin ordered a mandatory evacuation. I headed
for I-10 with my wife and her mother in the car. Her father had
stayed behind, never to be seen again. I heard there were more than
one hundred people missing after the storm and he was one of them.
It took us three days, but after eating, sleeping, and praying in the
car, we finally made it to my cousin's house in Laurel (Mississippi).
My brother and his family had waited too long to get out. They
couldn't even get to the Superdome. Two days after the storm they
had to be rescued from the rising floodwaters. It was two months
before I heard from him again. They ended up in Houston, Texas.*

SURVIVOR FROM NEW ORLEANS

INTRODUCTION

For most of the millions of people in the storm's path, Hurricane Katrina was a traumatic, life-altering event. Over the weekend of August 27 and 28, uncertainty regarding the projected track of the storm was transformed into ever-increasing anxiety as it churned northward through the Gulf. On that fateful Sunday morning, area residents awoke to learn that their worst fears were justified and time was running out. Authorities belatedly issued calls for mandatory evacuations, a process that would strain the nerves and stretch the resources of those in the projected path of destruction. People dealt with the arduous tasks of determining destinations, arranging transportation, obtaining needed funds, locating important records and documents, calming fellow family members, and reassuring worried relatives.

As evacuation efforts progressed, pressing questions emerged: Where will we go? How long will we be gone? To what will we return? Others faced a significantly more urgent question: If we can't get out, what will happen to me and my family when Katrina hits? This chapter provides aggregate answers to the questions Katrina survivors faced. We organize this information as follows: 1) evacuation behaviors of the general population; 2) outcomes for those attempting to shelter in place; 3) issues of family safety and separation; 4) the extent, causes, and patterns of residential property damage; 5) post-storm population displacement; 6) financial costs and effects; and 7) issues of exposure to hazardous wastes. For many of these topics, we also provide demographic comparisons that reveal extensive disparities in disaster vulnerabilities and outcomes.

EVACUATION

Weather forecasters and emergency management officials began to encourage residents to voluntarily evacuate as early as Friday, August 26, three days prior to Hurricane Katrina's landfall on the following Monday. However, authorities did not issue a mandatory evacuation order until Sunday morning, just one day before landfall. While most residents ultimately heeded this call, there were many who either did not or could not evacuate. There is general consensus that emergency management authorities' handling of the evacuation was inept and ineffective. Likewise, the public's response was slow and inadequate. These shortcomings, which contributed significantly to the storm's destruction and trauma, were the result of a number of factors: (1) the lateness of the National Hurricane Center projection for

FIGURE 2.1. New Orleans residents line up to seek shelter in the Superdome on Friday before the storm. Federal Emergency Management Agency (FEMA), photo by Marty Bahamonde.

TABLE 2.1. Individual storm experiences

Which of the following best describes your
experience with the storm itself?

	Full sample	MS	LA
Evacuated prior to storm	79%	63%	86%
Rescued during storm	2	1	2
Stayed in the home	18	35	11
Don't know/No answer	1	1	1
Total	100%	100%	100%
Total number of respondents	2511	802	1709

landfall; (2) hesitation in issuing a general mandatory evacuation order; (3) fatigue due to previous hurricane "false alarms"; (4) the inability of some residents to evacuate, especially in New Orleans, where it is estimated that 112,000 people lacked personal transportation;[1] and (5) the missed opportunities evident in the thousands of unused seats on planes, trains, and buses departing the target areas. Thus, while most residents did evacuate, many thousands stayed. Estimates from the greater New Orleans area suggest that some 150,000 to 200,000 people were either unwilling or unable to leave prior to the storm, a major factor in the loss of life and personal injury.[2]

Nevertheless, as shown in table 2.1, four out of five residents in our sample did leave the area prior to Katrina's Monday landfall. However, the survey also reveals that the evacuation pattern varied significantly by state, with Mississippi residents reporting only a 63 percent evacuation rate and Louisiana residents reporting an 86 percent rate.

This variation may reflect the fact that as late as Sunday morning, weather forecasters were projecting a direct hit for New Orleans. This projection, and a primary media focus on the city's vulnerability, may have led many Mississippi residents to believe that the impact would be less severe in their area. In fact, after initially making landfall just south of Buras, Louisiana, Hurricane Katrina did veer slightly toward the east, but this placed the Mississippi Gulf Coast in the northeasterly quadrant of the storm, the area with the most destructive force. As a result, Mississippi coastal residents who stayed ultimately faced a massive and destructive twenty-eight-foot storm surge.

Individual storm experiences also differed by location and by race. Although differences in the percentages of whites and blacks who evacuated prior to the storm were minimal, there were significant differences in the experiences of those who attempted to shelter in place. While less than 1 percent of the whites who stayed in their homes were subsequently rescued during the storm, almost 6 percent of the African Americans who stayed had to be rescued. In addition, some of the racial differences are obscured by the differences between the two states. While there were virtually no racial differences in evacuation rates in Mississippi, Louisiana blacks were 7 percent more likely than whites to attempt to shelter in place.

Also, while blacks were twice as likely as whites to have been rescued during the storm in Mississippi, blacks in Louisiana were seven times more likely than whites to have been rescued. Thus, a considerably greater number of African Americans endured Katrina's high winds, storm surge, and subsequent flooding to the point that they required rescue. Although the actual percentages may seem small, in fact they represent thousands of whites and tens of thousands of African Americans in the area that Katrina devastated.

What accounts for these racial disparities? They were due primarily to the lower socioeconomic status and associated vulnerabilities of the African Americans living in the path of the storm. Income disparities would affect evacuation decisions in several ways. Those with lower incomes had fewer transportation options for leaving the area. As noted above, it has been estimated that over one hundred thousand people in the greater New Orleans area were without any personal means of transportation, essentially being stranded. Plus, even if those in the lower income brackets could arrange automobile transportation, they would have had much more difficulty managing expenses on the road such as gasoline, food, and lodging. Added to this was a lack of other readily available transportation options, such as buses, trains, and airplanes, and even where such options were available, their use was often precluded by the cost of tickets. Thus, for the tens of thousands of African American residents who did not have the capacity to leave their homes, the governmental failure to promptly and efficiently facilitate evacuation amounted to abandonment in the face of catastrophe.

FAMILY SEPARATION AND SAFETY

Hurricane Katrina not only caused a massive movement of people out of their homes, but also disrupted and fragmented families and key social relationships. This immediate and important social consequence of the storm

FIGURE 2.2. A central location in the Houston Astrodome for organizing efforts to reunite parents with missing children, September 2, 2005. FEMA, photo by Andrea Booher.

produced heightened levels of stress and anxiety resulting from isolation and concern for the safety of separated family members. Many separations occurred when more vulnerable family members, such as children and the elderly, were sent away for their own protection, while other family members chose to shelter in place. In addition, emergency management authorities often compelled separations through their decisions to concentrate initial rescue efforts on women, children, and the elderly. Both during and after the storm, separations also occurred when family members who left to seek help were unable to return due to road conditions, gas shortages, and curfews.

In some cases, families were aware of the locations of separated members and were able to maintain at least occasional contact throughout the ordeal. While those types of separations are by definition stressful, they could hardly be compared to the cases where there were complete communication breakdowns such that the circumstances and even the very survival of separated family members remained unknown for extended periods of time.

Regardless of the causes, the extent of these separations was shocking. The National Center for Missing and Exploited Children, just one of several organizations involved in efforts to reunite families separated during Hurricane Katrina and its aftermath, reported that just over five thousand children in Louisiana, Alabama, and Mississippi were categorized as "missing/

displaced children or 'children looking for parents.'"[3] When considering the effects of such separations, it is important to recognize that children may be more susceptible to post-traumatic stress disorders than adults.[4] Even after being reunited, children may continue to suffer negative consequences from disruption of their normal routines, especially their recreational and educational activities. This is especially the case for children whose families were displaced for extended periods of time.[5]

Measuring separation and safety concerns of family members was accomplished for our sample with direct questions regarding respondents' experiences and perceptions. The key question dealt with whether or not the respondent had been separated from any other family members because of Katrina. Incredibly, as shown in table 2.2, more than half of those we surveyed experienced such separations. People from Louisiana were considerably more likely to have experienced family separations than those in Mississippi, likely due to the lower proportion of evacuations in Mississippi. Nonetheless, this collective picture is tragic, and our data clearly reveal that African Americans suffered a disproportionate share of these disruptive experiences. While slightly over half of whites were separated from family members, over two-thirds of African American families endured traumatic separations. Clearly, loss of contact with family members produced constant worry and fear, culminating in a post-storm context of maximum distress for survivors.

In assessing the negative consequences of family separation and safety issues, it is important to be mindful of the significant variation in the causes and conditions of the separations. Family members who voluntarily separated and maintained contact during and after the storm would experience

TABLE 2.2. Separated from family

Were you separated from any of your family members because of the storm?

	Full sample	MS	LA
Yes	55.9%	39.7%	63.5%
No	43.4	59.9	35.7
No family	0.5	0.5	0.5
Don't know/No answer	0.2	—	0.3
Total	100.0%	100.0%	100.0%
Total number of respondents	802	1709	2511

stress, but not nearly to the extent of those whose family members went missing in the chaos of the storm for extensive and indefinite periods of time. While our survey did not directly address such variations in separation, we do have an indirect measure. We asked whether the respondent was ever unsure about the safety of any family members during or after the storm. The data reveal that almost half of the sample experienced such uncertainty, and on this issue, results vary little by state. Clearly, this was a significant source of anxiety and stress for almost one out of every two residents of our target area. When analyzed separately by race, 44 percent of whites and 59 percent of blacks were uncertain about the safety of separated family members. Thus, as was the case with evacuation trauma, African Americans suffered a disproportionate burden of such anxiety-producing circumstances.

RESIDENTIAL DAMAGE

When Hurricane Katrina pummeled the Mississippi coast, residents experienced wind, flooding, and a massive storm surge that moved up to twelve miles inland. While the wind and initial storm surge were not quite as intense in Louisiana, the overtopping, undercutting, and ultimate collapse of levees left thousands of homes underwater for days or weeks after the storm. As a result, a substantial number of homes were either totally destroyed or damaged to the point that they were not habitable. The question arises: What was the extent of residential damage in the impact area in the wake of Hurricane Katrina?

As table 2.3 shockingly reveals, Katrina's wrath annihilated the built environment—only 4 percent of our respondents' homes suffered no damage, while almost one in seven homes was totally destroyed. Residential damage levels across Louisiana and Mississippi were similar, clearly revealing the massive structural devastation caused by Katrina over a broad geographic area. Given these findings, the most immediate and dramatic impact of Katrina's fury was residential destruction and, in the aftermath, widespread homelessness.

Results on reported storm damage are even more informative when contrasted by race. Although absolute numbers are small, whites were almost twice as likely as African Americans to have suffered little or no damage, whereas African Americans were almost twice as likely to have had their homes totally destroyed. Undoubtedly, these findings reflect preexisting socioeconomic vulnerabilities that resulted in African American homes

FIGURE 2.3. Aerial view of homes tossed about by Katrina's storm surge in Port Sulphur, Louisiana. NOAA Aviation Weather Center, photo by Commander Mark Moran, and Lieutenants Phil Eastman and Dave Demers, NOAA Aircraft Operations Center.

TABLE 2.3. Self-reported storm damage

Thinking of your residence when Katrina hit, which of the following best describes the damage from the storm?

	Full sample	*MS*	*LA*
No damage	3.7%	2.2%	4.4%
Minor damage	25.4	23.2	26.5
Moderate damage	27.4	31.7	25.3
Major damage	29.7	28.8	30.2
Totally destroyed	13.6	14.0	13.4
Don't know/No answer	0.1	0.1	0.2
Total	100.0%	100.0%	100.0%
Total number of respondents	802	1709	2511

being more commonly located in flood-prone areas, as well as the likelihood that home construction in lower socioeconomic neighborhoods would be less able to withstand the violent impact of Katrina's wind and water. These socioeconomic vulnerabilities contribute, in a cumulative fashion, to the negative effects on African Americans.

TABLE 2.4. Source of storm damage

Was the primary damage to your home due to _____?

	Full sample	MS	LA
Wind	54.7%	64.5%	50.0%
Storm surge	3.6	5.2	2.8
Flooding	18.9	6.9	24.7
Combination	22.1	22.4	21.9
Don't know/No answer	0.8	0.9	0.7
Total	100.0%	100.0%	100.0%
Total number of respondents	2417	784	1633

The primary contributing factors for this extensive damage pattern involved the triple menace of a hurricane: intense sustained and gusting winds, a massive wind-driven storm surge overtopped with crashing waves, and widespread post-storm flooding. The built environment in Katrina's path suffered extensively from all three of these factors. However, our survey revealed that the primary causes of residential damage varied by state. On the one hand, as seen in table 2.4, almost two of every three Mississippi residents reported that wind was the most dominant destructive force, while only 50 percent of Louisiana residents provided a similar assessment. This disparity was due to the geographical track of Hurricane Katrina, which subjected the Mississippi Gulf Coast to the most severe winds. On the other hand, Louisiana residents were three times more likely to identify flooding as the primary source of major damage from the storm, reflecting the massive post-storm flooding that inundated 80 percent of New Orleans. The next largest category includes the combined effects of wind, surge, and flooding, and at slightly more than one in five, the numbers in this category are very similar across both states.

These aggregate data obscure an important relationship between the source and the extent of the damage. While wind generally appears to be the greatest culprit when it comes to damage, a more complete picture can be gained by looking at the cause of damage at each level of damage intensity. Although the data are not presented in tabular form, wind did indeed cause a lot of minor and moderate damage, but major damage and total destruction were much more likely to have been caused by the storm surge and flooding. Where homes were totally destroyed or suffered major damage, storm surge and flooding were identified as the primary source of destruction by four out of five respondents. This finding for survivors clearly reinforces the premise that water is the foremost destroyer of the built environment when hurricanes make landfall.

FINANCIAL EFFECTS

Another critical measure of stress for survivors involved the direct financial consequences of Katrina. To get at this issue, we asked respondents two rather straightforward questions. One dealt with net dollar losses (after grants or insurance reimbursements) from all sources, including lost wages and lost profits from a business. The other was an estimate of the out-of-pocket expenses for replacing or repairing their homes. Although many of the respondents were unwilling (or unable) to make such estimates, among those who did, almost one-third declared that the storm was a huge drain on their personal financial resources.

As shown in table 2.5, when asked about their total losses from the storm, only 8 percent of the respondents reported that they lost nothing, while over one-half (54 percent) suffered losses of $25,000 or more. Furthermore, one of the most striking findings is that almost one-fourth of those who endured Katrina reported losses in excess of $100,000. Based upon these results, it is apparent that the hurricane delivered a serious financial blow to the overwhelming majority of affected residents.

Table 2.5 also reports out-of-pocket costs associated with repairing or rebuilding a damaged residence, a question asked only of homeowners. Despite reimbursements from insurance and funds from state grant programs, 43 percent of the respondents stated that they personally spent over $10,000 on their homes. Almost one of every three homeowners had out-of-pocket expenses that ranged from $25,000 to over $100,000, indicating that many of those affected had to spend significant amounts of their own money to make their residences livable.

Since racial disparities in the impact area of Katrina are of particular interest, we have also included racial breakdowns in table 2.5. Among the more regrettable findings in these comparisons is that while the net worth of African American families is significantly lower than that of whites, the percentage of blacks suffering total losses in the $25,000–$100,000 and over $100,000 ranges is significantly higher than that of whites. Thus, the proportional loss in net worth was drastically higher for African Americans than for whites. When it comes to racial disparities in out-of-pocket home

TABLE 2.5. Financial impact of storm

How much money have you personally spent "out-of-pocket" specifically to replace or repair your home? Next we want to get the total dollar value of your losses from Katrina. This would be your initial losses less any grants or insurance reimbursements. It would also include lost wages or profits from a business. What would you estimate your total loss to be?

	$ Home repair	Total $ loss	$ Home repair		Total $ loss	
	All in sample		White	AA	White	AA
Zero	15%	8%	15%	14%	9%	3%
Less than $10,000	42	21	45	34	22	16
$10,000 to $25,000	16	17	15	20	18	15
$25,000 to $100,000	21	32	19	28	30	39
Over $100,000	6	22	6	4	21	27
Total	100%	100%	100%	100%	100%	100%
Total number of respondents	1512	1825	1044	310	1267	338

repair costs, we find that 52 percent of black homeowners spent more than $10,000 while the comparable figure for whites was 40 percent. Exploring racial differences on these financial issues, however, is complicated by income differences between the two groups. With median household income for African Americans at about two-thirds that of whites, the actual impact of such losses fell much more heavily on black families. Thus, it is apparent that financial losses were strikingly higher for African Americans. Once again, the consequences of Katrina were a more intense burden for blacks.

Another important dimension of Hurricane Katrina's debilitating financial impact was the extent to which these costs and losses were considered to be problems by those who were affected. To investigate this issue, we asked respondents to provide their assessments of the financial distress they experienced due to the storm. While these findings are not reported in tabular form, we found that more than three-fourths of the sample acknowledged some level of financial difficulty, with one-fourth characterizing their problems as severe. When contrasted by state and race, minimal differences were observed between Louisiana and Mississippi, but once again there were significant differences between whites and African Americans. The percentage of African Americans reporting severe financial problems was more than double that of whites (44 percent versus 19 percent). This observation reveals yet another source of post-Katrina stress and disruption where the burdens fell more heavily on African Americans.

From data collected five years after Katrina, a slightly different indicator of family financial distress revealed that some progress had been made over time. From 2008 to 2010, the number of people reporting that their financial problems from the hurricane were at an end had more than doubled. Even so, slightly over one-half of those in the impact area were still suffering financially five years after the storm, and one in ten characterized their ongoing financial problems as severe. Additionally, in 2010, African Americans were significantly more likely than whites to report continued financial difficulties and more than twice as likely to report severe problems. Thus, while some modest progress had been made in the two intervening years, the pace of economic recovery could be best characterized as slow and uneven, with African Americans suffering a disproportionate burden. These lingering financial impacts reflect the reality that the nightmare of Katrina did not end quickly, resulting in serious long-term money problems for survivors.

POST-STORM DISPLACEMENT

The initial displacement associated with Hurricane Katrina stemmed largely from the evacuation of residents prior to landfall. For many, this initial displacement transformed into long-term separation as people were either unable or unwilling to return to their homes. For many others, subsequent displacement occurred when they returned to find their homes uninhabitable. Given the catastrophic level of residential devastation and the extremely slow pace at which floodwaters receded from New Orleans, it is not surprising that in the days after the storm, tens of thousands of additional people were forced once again to leave their homes and move to shelters both in and out of the area, including out of state. Ultimately affecting over a half million people, this mass movement has been characterized as the largest displacement of Americans since the Civil War and significantly larger than the Dust Bowl of the 1930s.

Obviously, much of this displacement resulted from damage to homes caused by the storm, but in addition, the overall condition of neighborhoods contributed to dislocation. After the storm had passed, many neighborhoods, especially those in the New Orleans area, lacked the most basic services, including electricity, gas, water, sewage, and public transportation.

FIGURE 2.4. At the beginning of the post-storm diaspora, residents wait to be evacuated to parts unknown. Metairie, Louisiana, I-10 at Causeway Boulevard, August 31, 2005. Wikimedia Commons, photo by LSUsoccerbum.

In those neighborhoods, individual homes that were not seriously damaged were still uninhabitable due to overall neighborhood conditions. In many cases, residents voluntarily sought shelter elsewhere due to the conditions of their homes and neighborhoods, but in some cases, they were forced to leave by local authorities. In New Orleans, for example, Mayor Ray Nagin issued an order on September 7 (nine days after the storm) requiring the mandatory evacuation of all civilian residents of the city.[6] That order stayed in effect until September 29, when authorities initiated a process of reopening neighborhoods by zip code, beginning with unflooded areas of Algiers, the Central Business District, the French Quarter, and Uptown. The process of reopening areas to allow residents to return home dragged on for months.

Thus, for many Katrina survivors, the habitability of their former residences was the critical question. Upon their return, would they be able to resume life in their homes and neighborhoods? To tap this dimension of residential damage, respondents were asked specifically whether their homes were habitable after the storm. Tragically, over 60 percent of our respondents returned to find that they were not able to live in their homes. These results varied by state, with four in ten residents forced to move from their homes in Mississippi, while the comparable figure in Louisiana was seven in ten.

As with other important measures, racial breakdowns regarding displacement reveal important disparities. As displayed in table 2.6, whites were more than twice as likely as African Americans to have been able to stay in their homes after the storm. Part of this pattern was due to the geographical location of some African American homes in flood-prone areas and the cheaper architecture and cut-rate construction techniques used to build housing in the poor neighborhoods where many blacks lived. Large tracts of affordable housing that had been home to lower-income African Americans were either destroyed by the storm or flooded, condemned, and demolished afterward. In addition, many housing projects serving poor blacks were closed after the storm, further contributing to their displacement throughout the impact area, but especially in New Orleans. Once again these and other findings make clear that African Americans suffered a disproportionate burden of damage and displacement, resulting in significant disadvantages for individual, family, neighborhood, and community recovery.

In summary, hundreds of thousands of people had their lives massively disrupted by Hurricane Katrina. Obviously, such disruptions, even for the short term, are not only terribly inconvenient but also can be extremely stressful. And although the displacement may have been short-lived for some, large numbers of Katrina survivors were out of their homes for extended periods, and many never returned to their pre-Katrina residences. We will more fully investigate these issues in the following chapter.

TABLE 2.6. Residential habitability, by race

Did you continue to live in your home after the storm, or did you have to move out?

	All in sample	White	African American
Stayed in residence	38.6%	44.8%	21.1%
Had to move	60.8	54.8	78.3
Don't know/No answer	0.6	0.4	0.6
Total	100.0%	100.0%	100.0%
Total number of respondents	2511	1634	506

Another source of stress involved the extent to which people believed that they or their family members had been exposed to dangerous chemicals due to the storm, as well as the extent to which such exposure continued due to the presence of such chemicals in their neighborhoods. Such concerns were well justified.

When Katrina's huge storm surge came inland, it upset and overturned millions of containers of hazardous household materials, including gasoline, oil, pesticides, fertilizers, paints, solvents, and cleaning agents of all kinds. There was additional spillage of oil, grease, battery acid, and gasoline from the estimated four hundred thousand vehicles, including cars, buses, trucks, boats, etc., that were underwater during the storm surge and subsequent flooding. Added to this was human waste in sewage overflows and decomposing animals, including innumerable pets and rodents that drowned in the storm. As if that were not enough, according to an EPA report, the storm surge flooded eighteen Superfund National Priority List sites and more than four hundred industrial facilities where hazardous materials were being stored or managed.[7] As floodwaters receded, they left behind countless tons of hazardous substances in sediments throughout Louisiana and Mississippi.

To explore the concern over chemical exposure, respondents were asked to agree or disagree with the following statement: "I believe that either myself or my family members have been exposed to dangerous chemicals because of Katrina." Results reveal that more than a third of respondents (35 percent) agreed with the statement. When focusing the question on conditions at the time of the survey, 21 percent agreed with the following statement: "I worry that there are dangerous chemicals in my neighborhood." Concern over dangerous chemical exposure did not diminish over time. Indeed, anxiety over exposure to toxic chemicals actually increased. In 2010, 37 percent believed that they or their family members had been exposed, while 24 percent acknowledged continued worry over dangerous chemicals still lurking in their neighborhoods.

The long-term effects of stress and anxiety over such exposure will negatively affect the mental health of Katrina survivors for decades to come. That consequence, however, is only part of the puzzle. The actual physical health effects of exposure are also likely to adversely affect residents well into the future. Both the physical and mental health effects of Hurricane Katrina are investigated more fully in later chapters.

THE LONG ROAD HOME
RETURN, REUNIFICATION, AND THE INFAMOUS FEMA TRAILER

*I guess I can talk to you now, but when we lived in Renaissance
Village, we couldn't do no interviews, not unless there was a FEMA
person there. And what you gonna say in front of a FEMA person?
You'd be afraid they'd kick you out if you told somebody the truth.
And truth was, that place weren't fit for man nor beast. I don't know
what was worse, the stink of the sewer or the stink of the chemicals in
the trailer. I guess the chemicals 'cause of what it does to your lungs.
I was up coughing half the night on most nights. And the days weren't
much better, what with the kids running wild 'cause they had nothing
to do. A lot of my neighbors just sat around reading their Bibles most
of the time, waiting for deliverance. Didn't seem to help them much
'cause when they closed the place down, most of them had nowhere
to go. When I came back to New Orleans, my old house was just fine,
but I couldn't live there 'cause they had raised the rent . . . more than
double. I'm living with my cousin now. But he's just about done with
me. Ha ha. I just don't know what's next. I guess I got to pray on it.*

NEW ORLEANS RESIDENT, RECENTLY RETURNED
FROM RENAISSANCE VILLAGE (A FEMA TRAILER
PARK NEAR BATON ROUGE)

INTRODUCTION

In this chapter, we review patterns and trends associated with the first steps
in community recovery from the extraordinary devastation and displacement caused by Hurricane Katrina. Typically, the disaster recovery period
is a time during which the physical damage and disruption of the event
are assessed, addressed, and reversed. At the community level, recovery

includes the return of residents, the reuniting of families, the reestablishment of daily routines, and the general restoration of community life. As we shall see in this chapter, the pace of such recovery has been painfully slow, and it has occurred unevenly across different geographic areas and demographic groups.

We begin our assessment of recovery by examining how long it took people to return to their homes. We also document the housing status of residents before and after the storm, specifically homeownership versus renting, as well as comparative assessments of pre-Katrina residences with post-Katrina accommodations. Next, we expand upon our previously reported findings on family separation to include the time it took people to reunite with their families after the storm. Finally, since the provision of FEMA trailers became such an infamous component of the post-storm response, we provide an analysis of the extent and duration of respondents' experiences with this controversial temporary housing.

When interpreting our findings in these areas, one limitation is evident. Given that the geographical target for the interviews was the major impact area of the storm, as a practical matter there was no viable option to include the tens of thousands of Katrina survivors who did not return to the area after the storm.[1] Surely, many of those survivors were among the group that had endured the most stressful and lengthy family separations. Thus, our findings clearly understate the magnitude of the overall disruption resulting from Hurricane Katrina. In addition, those who never returned to this devastated area could not contribute to the recovery of their communities. Since we cannot measure the potential contribution they might have made had they returned, the picture we present here is limited to that of residents who were sufficiently capable and motivated to return, assess, and commit to reestablishing their homes, neighborhoods, and communities. The result is perhaps a slightly distorted, though nevertheless telling and chilling, picture of post-Katrina conditions.

TO RETURN HOME, OR NOT?

Undoubtedly, Hurricane Katrina generated one of the largest displacements of people in US history. This population shift was unplanned, rapid, and traumatic. The initial evacuation of approximately 1.2 million people was compounded and extended by post-storm conditions. In New Orleans, because of post-storm flooding and the absence of habitable accommodations, all those who did not evacuate prior to the storm were eventually

FIGURE 3.1. Neighborhood conditions months after the storm included nightmarish pest-infested debris piles. Port Sulphur, Louisiana, December 2, 2005. FEMA, photo by Marvin Nauman.

forced to leave by order of Mayor Nagin, effective September 7, 2005. Thus, by the end of the first week in September, the city was a virtual ghost town. As mentioned earlier, authorities did not begin the process of allowing residents to return to New Orleans until a month after the storm, and even then, permission was granted on a neighborhood-by-neighborhood basis over a period of several months. This process was slow and agonizing for residents.

Even though forced post-storm evacuations were not mandated in other areas of Louisiana and Mississippi, the lack of basic services and other accessibility issues, including debris removal, road and bridge repair, and disruption of utility services, kept many other people from returning to their homes for days and weeks after the storm. In this way, the coordination of recovery activities often defied individual preferences. The stress and uncertainty associated with this process haunted many residents for many months after the storm.

Given the many attendant complications, no exact count of displaced persons exists. Estimates of the ultimate total of the displaced before, during, and after the storm range from 1.2 to 2 million people. Perhaps the most definitive source is the Bureau of Labor Statistics Current Population Study, which places this figure at 1.5 million.[2] But the estimates leave aside

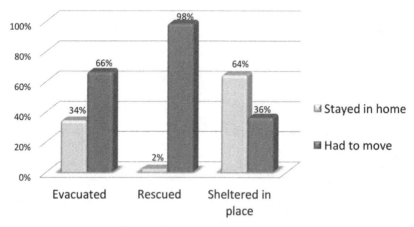

FIGURE 3.2. Breakdown of storm experience by post-storm displacement.

a question of critical importance: How long did this displacement last? We provide an answer with information about the extent and duration of residential displacement, including variations by state of residence and race.

As noted earlier, almost 80 percent of our survey respondents evacuated prior to Hurricane Katrina's landfall. Over 60 percent of those found their homes uninhabitable upon their return. While these figures attest to the magnitude of displacement, they do not provide a full and clear representation of the dynamics of this massive population shift. Of course, not everyone who evacuated prior to the storm should be considered "displaced." In addition, many who did not evacuate were subsequently displaced due to their inability to remain in their homes after Katrina. Insights into these issues are revealed below.

Figure 3.2 reveals several important descriptive findings. First, among those who initially evacuated, two-thirds could not return immediately to their homes, which ultimately extended the duration of their displacements. Second, only one of the forty-four people who were rescued during the storm was able to stay at home after the storm. In addition, of those who were able to stay in their homes during the storm, more than one-third (36 percent) subsequently had to move out. If we combine those who evacuated with those who did not evacuate but were forced to move after the storm, we find that 88 percent of our respondents experienced some sort of residential displacement. Indeed, Katrina's initial impact uprooted and redistributed the survivors in an unprecedented manner.

As noted above, slightly more than 60 percent of our respondents reported that they had to move after the storm. To elaborate on the impact of that fact, those respondents were asked how long after the storm they had to wait before they were able to return to their homes. The average time these residents were displaced was about ten months. Table 3.1 displays the results by category, with the largest category (37 percent) of residents being out of their homes for between one and six months, and a full one-fifth of the sample having never returned to their original pre-storm residences. When looking at length of time out of the home by state, the most striking finding is that three years after the storm, one in three Mississippi residents had not moved back to their pre-Katrina homes. These results make it apparent that the residential damage suffered by almost a third of the respondents residing in Harrison and Hancock Counties in Mississippi was so severe that it precluded any hope of rebuilding and returning to their homes. The homes were gone forever—permanent casualties of Katrina.

When making comparisons by race, once again we find that African Americans shared a disproportionate burden. For example, blacks were displaced on average for more than a year (12.2 months), while whites were displaced for well less than a year (9.2 months). Thus, in addition to suffering more extensive residential destruction and proportionately more family separation, African Americans also suffered significantly longer residential displacement than whites. Once again, the cumulative consequences of these experiences cannot be quantified, but they certainly seriously compound the detrimental impacts of the storm.

When interpreting these results, it is important to keep in mind that our sample included those people who were currently residing in the storm-

TABLE 3.1. Time out of home

How long was it after the storm before
you returned to live in your home?

	Full sample	*MS*	*LA*
Less than one month	11%	13%	10%
One to six months	37	23	41
Seven to twelve months	17	20	16
Over one year	13	11	14
Never moved back	20	32	17
Don't know/No answer	2	2	2
Total	100%	100%	100%
Total number of respondents	1542	333	1209

affected area. As noted above, it did not include those who were displaced to various places across the country. If we combine the 20 percent of our sample who never moved back to their pre-storm residence with the untold number of those who left the area for good, we can conclude that a very large proportion of the original residents of our study area are gone, never to return. This conclusion is confirmed by many other research studies and aggregated population data. A number of characteristics of Katrina contributed to this dire situation. Obviously, financial hardships explain part of the outcome.

Looking at comparisons of residential damage and financial problems, we find that 38 percent of those experiencing major damage had severe financial problems, as did 52 percent of those whose homes were totally destroyed. Thus, 90 percent of those whose homes suffered the most damage experienced severe financial hardship. Such untoward circumstances likely precluded any option for these families to return and rebuild their pre-Katrina residences.

Many neighborhoods, especially in New Orleans, were never reconstituted with basic municipal services. As a result, these neighborhoods were uninhabitable for more than a decade, and many are likely to remain so indefinitely. Many neighborhoods in the affected areas also included disproportionate numbers of rental properties. Without the bond of homeownership, such neighborhoods were relatively easy to abandon, further contributing to the depopulation of the region. Estimates suggest that at the height of this diaspora, as many as 1.2 million Katrina survivors were scattered around the country in cities such as Baton Rouge, Dallas, Houston, Little Rock, and Atlanta; others were moved as far away as Los Angeles, Las Vegas, and even Alaska. The most common destination was Houston, which accepted over two hundred thousand evacuees, primarily from New Orleans. Two weeks after the storm, the *Washington Post* reported that one-half of those who went to Houston had already decided to settle in that city rather than return to their pre-Katrina homes.[3] For many, staying away was an easy decision to make. For starters, the costs of returning, including transportation and relocation expenses, were often beyond their means. But perhaps more importantly, few of them had jobs or homes to which they could return. In all too many instances, their previous neighborhoods and their means of livelihood had been both physically and socially eliminated.

A final factor in the decision not to return relates to the hectic hurricane seasons of 2004 and 2005. There were sixteen named storms in 2004, including Ivan, a major hurricane which made landfall in the Florida panhandle, followed in 2005 by twenty-seven named storms, including

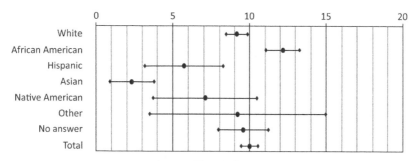

FIGURE 3.3. Distribution of length of time (in months) before returning home, by race/ethnicity.

four hurricanes that made landfall along the northern Gulf Coast (Cindy, Dennis, Katrina, and Rita). This rather unprecedented sequence of storms led many to believe that climate change was driving increases in hurricane activity and intensity, and that many more massive storms could be expected to devastate the Gulf Coast. While subsequent hurricane seasons have not lived up to such grim expectations, this was undoubtedly a widespread concern as evacuees confronted the decision of whether to return to their communities.

In figure 3.3, we provide a comparison across racial and ethnic groups of the length of time respondents were out of their homes. This figure includes the confidence interval (95 percent) as part of the plot to illustrate both the distribution of displacement duration from primary residences and the range of displacement time. The mean duration (the central point on the line) provides the average in months, but the reality of displacement is more readily understood in terms of a range of time. Some residents were able to return sooner than average, while others took considerably longer than average to return home. The significant differences between African Americans, Hispanics, and whites are also apparent (note that where there is overlap among other group ranges, these three groups do not overlap). Once again, African Americans suffered disproportionately from Katrina; they were displaced from their pre-Katrina residences for significantly longer on average than other racial and ethnic groups.

As a follow-up to these findings, in the 2010 survey, respondents still living in their pre-Katrina residences were asked about the condition of their homes. Approximately five years after the storm, more than one-fourth of them stated that they were still residing in damaged residences. For Katrina survivors, living in such homes provided a constant reminder of the destruction wreaked by the storm. This has surely prolonged the psychological distress associated with experiencing Katrina and precluded a return to social normalcy.

Another important aspect of community recovery involves the pre- and post-Katrina housing status of residents. The good news is that by the time of our initial survey in 2008, approximately 80 percent of the sample had returned to the homes they lived in prior to Katrina, even though, as noted above, many of those homes were still damaged. If, however, we focus on the 20 percent who were forced to move to some other residence, we find that these respondents were worse off according to three critical measures: housing status, homeownership, and comparative assessments of pre-Katrina housing with post-Katrina accommodations.

Among the subgroup of the sample who did not return to their pre-Katrina residences, only 73 percent of those who lived in single-family homes prior to Katrina were able to move to single-family homes elsewhere after the storm; 27 percent had to make other arrangements. Among that group, 15 percent moved into apartments, 5 percent into mobile homes, and 4 percent still lived in FEMA trailers. These findings are also reflected in a comparison of homeownership versus renting before and after the storm. Among the homeowners who did not return to their pre-Katrina residence, 73 percent reported owning their homes at the time of the 2008 survey. Another 20 percent were renting their residences, and 5 percent were living rent-free in FEMA trailers. Needless to say, having to move from home-owner to renter status added to individual and family hardships, both emotionally and financially.

As noted above, three years after the storm, approximately one in five residents in our sample had not returned to their original homes. While one might hope that a silver lining of the storm would be the replacement of older housing stock with newer, improved accommodations, only 41 percent of those who did not return to their pre-storm homes reported that their post-Katrina housing was nicer than the homes they had lived in prior to the storm. Almost one-third of this subgroup of the sample (31.6 percent) reported that their post-Katrina residence was not as nice as their original home, another finding that confirms a continued pattern of residential decline for those who were displaced by the storm.

One final concern regarding long-term residential displacement involves the extent to which housing patterns changed between 2008 and 2010. While we are able to make only limited comparisons, one of the more important issues involves the return to pre-Katrina homes. In the 2008 survey, 81.5 percent of our respondents reported living in the same residence where they had lived prior to Katrina. While exact figures are not available, many of the remaining 18.5 percent were still in temporary housing. Among that group, for example, a subsequent question revealed that 4 percent were still living in FEMA trailers; many others were renting apartments and mobile homes. Thus, many of those who were still out of their pre-Katrina homes in 2008 could conceivably have completed repairs and returned to their pre-Katrina homes by 2010. Unfortunately, this potential was not realized. In 2010, 81.6 percent reported living in their pre-Katrina homes, an inconsequential increase of .01 percent from two years earlier. This very disturbing trend clearly reveals the agonizingly slow pace of recovery for a significant minority of the residents affected by Katrina.

REUNITING WITH FAMILY

In addition to the death and destruction resulting from the storm, one of the most distressing and challenging consequences of Hurricane Katrina was the extended separations endured by family members. As noted in the previous chapter, approximately 56 percent of our sample reported having been separated from family members as a result of the storm. As a critical measure of recovery, those individuals were asked how long their separations lasted. Table 3.2 reveals that among the subgroup of the sample that experienced family separations, the most common separations lasted between one and six months, with 45 percent of our respondents falling into that category. However, two-thirds of this subgroup endured family separations of a month or more, and almost one in ten were still separated three years after the storm.

TABLE 3.2. Length of time separated from family

How long did this separation last?

	Full sample	*MS*	*LA*
Less than one month	29%	55%	21%
One to six months	45	32	49
Seven to twelve months	10	8	11
Over one year	4	2	5
Still separated	9	1	11
Don't know/No answer	3	2	3
Total	100%	100%	100%
Total number of respondents	2488	1085	1403

Analyzing data on family separation, we found significant variations by state. In Mississippi over one-half (55 percent) of families were reunited within a month; the comparable figure for Louisiana was only 20 percent. Approximately 12 percent of the separations among Mississippi respondents lasted more than six months, while more than one-quarter of the Louisiana respondents endured separations of that length. Even more disturbing, in Louisiana 11 percent of families were still separated at the time of the 2008 survey, while in Mississippi the comparable figure was only 1 percent.

Additional breakdowns (not shown here) reveal that African Americans were almost three times as likely as whites to suffer separations of more than six months, and more than twice as likely to still be separated from family members at the time of the 2008 survey. These observations further confirm the pattern of additional Katrina-related burdens endured by African Americans living in the area of impact.

While some might suggest that the magnitude of this unfortunate consequence of Katrina strains credibility, such findings are echoed in other studies of Katrina's effects. For example, based upon a survey of Red Cross applicants, Gallup estimated that six weeks after the storm more than one hundred thousand Katrina victims were still separated from family members, a figure that included about fifteen thousand parents who were separated from their children.[4] Regrettably, a number of these separations continued for many years after the storm. An internet search for "Katrina survivors united" yields hundreds of human-interest news stories about family reunifications that continued to occur for many years after the storm.

Once again, it is important to note that our survey does not tell the full story. For example, our measures of family separation only include human family members. For many families, the loss of a beloved pet can be equally traumatic, and, sadly, such separations were very common. The Louisiana Society for the Prevention of Cruelty to Animals estimated that of the 15,500 animals rescued during the storm, only about 15 to 20 percent were ever reunited with their owners.[5] Unfortunately, the doubt and uncertainty of family separation is an ongoing misfortune for some Katrina survivors, but the full extent of the problem remains unknown. From the outset of the disaster, controversy has brewed over the numbers of dead and missing. For example, there will never be agreement over the final body count, and no official list of those still missing exists. Katrina's wrath defies an accurate empirical accounting of the most basic information on the life-and-death consequences of the storm.

"TEMPORARY" HOUSING: FEMA TRAILERS

As we have seen, the devastation caused by Katrina resulted in significant displacement of large numbers of residents for lengthy periods of time. To ameliorate this problem in the short run, state and local officials offered emergency housing in apartments, motels, and hotels. But as the duration of displacement increased, some residents whose homes suffered major damage or outright destruction were provided temporary housing by the federal government in the form of small, self-contained travel trailers. According to the federal government, within the first year after the storm, FEMA had provided over one hundred thousand travel trailers to displaced residents in Louisiana, Mississippi, and Alabama.[6] This form of temporary housing came to be known as the infamous "FEMA trailer," and over the years it became clear that the term "temporary" was in the eye of the beholder.

Complaints about foul-smelling fumes in these trailers began to surface immediately. Subsequently, it was determined that the smell came from formaldehyde gas leeching from the particleboard used in construction of the trailers, and that people living in the trailers were being exposed to dangerous amounts of these toxic fumes with potentially harmful long-term health effects. As reported by the Centers for Disease Control, air quality tests of the trailers found formaldehyde concentrations at levels that have been linked to increased long-term risks of negative health effects, including certain types of cancers.[7] Even at minimally elevated levels, formaldehyde causes watering and burning eyes, nausea, and respiratory problems. Associated problems may be even worse for children, who have faster respiration, and elderly residents, who would likely spend more time inside the trailers. As a consequence, the length of time spent in a FEMA trailer became a critically important health concern for survivors.

Almost one in three people who were displaced from their homes reported that they had lived in a FEMA trailer at some point in time; that amounts to almost 20 percent of the overall sample. Even more alarming, many families lived in the trailers for extended periods of time, with the vast majority exposed to this toxic environment for many months. As presented in table 3.3, the largest proportion (34 percent) of trailer residents reported spending between seven and twelve months in these "temporary" housing units. Over 30 percent of those who lived in FEMA trailers did so for a year or longer. A closer look at the demographics of those in FEMA trailers reveals that African Americans were more likely than whites to have lived in one of the trailers. However, the actual duration of occupancy was similar across racial groups, suggesting modest racial disparity in the actual exposure to dangerous hazardous chemicals.

FIGURE 3.4. A sprawling FEMA trailer park in Biloxi, Mississippi, October 4, 2005. FEMA, photo by John Fleck.

TABLE 3.3. Time in a FEMA trailer

How long did you live in a FEMA trailer?

	Full sample	*MS*	*LA*
Less than one month	5%	3%	6%
One to six months	28	27	28
Seven to twelve months	34	31	35
Over one year	29	34	26
Still in trailer	3	2	3
Don't know/No answer	2	3	2
Total	100%	100%	100%
Total number of respondents	482	148	334

Given the supposed "temporary" nature of the shelter that FEMA trailers were intended to provide, these findings are especially discouraging for documenting community recovery. The duration of the use of FEMA trailers not only tends to confirm the excruciatingly slow pace of recovery but also makes evident a serious source of additional fear and stress. In answers to questions about exposure, 68 percent of respondents who lived in FEMA trailers believed that they or their family members had been exposed to dangerous chemicals as a result of the storm, while only 40 percent of respondents who did not live in the trailers believed this. Also, when considering the possible impact of formaldehyde exposure in FEMA trailers, it is important to note that the negative health consequences of extended exposure are generally unpredictable and may not manifest as health problems for years or even decades. Even if the actual health effects turn out to be minimal, the anxiety associated with possibly developing severe respiratory problems or cancers surely has had serious negative consequences for the emotional and psychological well-being of Katrina survivors.

The short-term effects of these experiences on the physical and mental health of residents will be elaborated in later chapters. The long-term effects will likely never be known with any degree of certainty, but one fact is apparent—these impacts were real, and the potential for serious long-term health consequences cannot be denied.

In this chapter, we have reviewed some of the major nonfinancial stressors for Katrina survivors. For those who have never had such experiences, it is hard to imagine the hardship and trauma that would result from losing one's home and being separated from loved ones. Although it took far too long, most families were ultimately reunited and their homes were rebuilt, but the anxiety associated with toxic exposure to cancer-causing chemicals will haunt some people for the rest of their lives. We expect that this will have detrimental consequences for the health and well-being of Katrina survivors. We will explore that in coming chapters, but first we will examine the additional sources of stress evident in survivors' attempts to seek insurance settlements and grant funds to rebuild their homes and resume their normal lives.

EMERGING OBSTACLES TO REBUILDING
INSURANCE CLAIMS AND GRANT PROGRAMS

*They called it the "Road Home Program," but it was actually
the "Road to Hell Program." We not only filed our application,
which was turned down, but we had to file for my wife's parents
and my parents. Between all the requirements, deadlines, and
conditions, no one has received a penny, and Katrina hit three
years ago. My father and mother lost all of their paperwork for
their older home, and it looks as if it will take forever to gather
original documents. My wife's parents gave up and moved to
Tennessee to live with their son—they just walked away from a
total loss and are still dealing with their homeowners' insurance.
The insurance adjusters are makeshift employees who have been
told to deny all claims and force victims to seek legal action. Of
course, the courts will take forever to make a decision. After months
and months of waiting, the insurance company said they didn't
have any of my paperwork, and I had to refile. I became part of
a lawsuit which includes many in our neighborhood. It seems as
though this will never end. Yes, we are on the "Road to Hell."*

SURVIVOR FROM NEW ORLEANS

INTRODUCTION

In this chapter we examine another important phase of recovery involv-
ing respondents' experiences in obtaining needed financial resources to repair and rebuild their homes. This recovery phase included four primary
sources of such funding: basic homeowners' insurance policies, National
Flood Insurance policies, the Mississippi Development Authority Hurricane Katrina Homeowner Assistance grants, and Louisiana Road Home

FIGURE 4.1. For many, the rebuilding process began with demolition. Keesler Air Force Base, one year after Katrina. US Air Force, photo by Kemberly Groue.

TABLE 4.1. Insurance claims and grant applications

Respondents who filed insurance claims and grant applications as a percentage of the overall sample.

	Full sample	**MS**	**LA**
Filed homeowners' claim	72%	74%	71%
Filed flood insurance claim	25%	11%	31%
Filed state grant application	31%	27%	32%
Total number of respondents	2511	802	1709

Program grants. Of course, these resources were only available to the subgroup of the sample who owned homes that sustained certain types of damage from the storm, but as can be seen in table 4.1, this constituted a relatively large proportion of residents in the impact area.

To identify respondents for whom these issues would be relevant, we asked those whose homes had sustained damage during the storm whether they had homeowners' or flood insurance and, if so, whether they had filed a claim. We also asked whether they had applied to a state grant program. Those who had filed insurance claims or grant applications were then asked about the status of their claims and grants. They were also asked to characterize the level of stress they had experienced in their attempts to obtain funding to repair or rebuild their homes through these means. Answers to these critical questions and their implications for recovery are presented in this chapter.

HOMEOWNERS' INSURANCE CLAIMS AND SETTLEMENTS

Among those respondents who suffered some amount of damage to their homes, 82 percent had homeowners' insurance, 93 percent of whom filed claims; as presented above, this subgroup constituted 72 percent of the overall sample. It should also be noted that while the process of resolving those claims contributed significantly to stress levels, respondents who suffered a significant loss from the storm and did not have homeowners' insurance were perhaps even more personally stressed. This number was not inconsequential, as 16 percent of homeowners who suffered losses from Katrina had no homeowners' insurance. Such circumstances surely contributed to some survivors simply walking away from homes that had sustained excessive damage.

Several factors contributed to the levels of stress involved in resolving homeowners' insurance claims. One of the most controversial issues involved the type of damage that a home had sustained. Homeowners' insurance policies typically include language that excludes flood damage from coverage. This exclusion was applied to both the huge storm surge that obliterated the Mississippi Gulf Coast and the post-Katrina flooding in the New Orleans area. Part of the rationale for this exclusion is that water damage in areas that had been identified as flood zones, as was the case throughout much of Katrina's impact area, would be eligible for coverage under the federal government's National Flood Insurance Program. If such were the case and the homeowner did not purchase such a policy, per the insurance companies' policies, any flood damage would be the homeowner's sole responsibility.

As noted in chapter 2, over one-half (55 percent) of our respondents attributed their residential damage to hurricane winds. The remaining 45 percent was split relatively evenly between those reporting water damage (whether from storm surge or flooding) and those reporting damage from a combination of wind and water. It should be noted that homeowners might be motivated by the exclusions in their policies to claim that their damage was caused by wind, rather than water. At the same time, insurance companies had strong incentives to assume that the damage was from water and was therefore excluded from coverage. Given these conflicting motivations, a definitive determination of the source of damage to a home became a very difficult and controversial process. This conflict was especially evident when all that was left of the home was the slab and scattered debris, an all-too-common occurrence across both Louisiana and Mississippi. In such cases, the question was whether the home had blown away or washed away. Resolving such questions certainly contributed to high levels of stress and anxiety for many Katrina survivors, leading to months of uncertainty.

Another complicating factor in this process involved the burden of proof. To determine the validity of a claim, did the homeowner have to prove that the home was destroyed by hurricane winds, or did the insurance company have to prove that water was the culprit? This issue cannot be settled legally; it varied by state, by insurance company, and by individual circumstances. Resolving these questions often forced homeowners into extended fights with their insurance companies, thereby creating additional uncertainty, anxiety, and stress.

Furthermore, homeowners were sometimes faced with questions regarding the sequence of events that led to the damage of their residences. Recall that slightly more than one in five homeowners reported damage that was the result of a combination of water and wind. If the wind ripped the roof off before the storm surge wiped the slab clean, the insurance company might still be liable for the roof damage. This possibility was potentially helpful to those homeowners who lacked flood insurance so that the only hope of any sort of settlement was from their basic homeowners' policy. However, with no eyewitnesses and evidence scattered for miles, proving the process and sequence of destruction became a most uncertain endeavor that favored the initial evaluations of insurance adjusters.

In most instances, the ultimate attribution of damage was in the hands of these insurance company "experts," who often had little credibility with homeowners. For some homeowners, the only alternative to an adverse finding was to take the insurance company to court, an approach that resulted in an extended period of uncertainty and an additional source of stress. In our survey, 7 percent of the full sample acknowledged being involved in a lawsuit as a result of the hurricane, while 11 percent refused to respond to that question. A common explanation for refusing to answer was that the respondent was not free to discuss such matters, suggesting that many of those who did not answer were also involved in litigation.

In addition to questions about noncovered damage, virtually all homeowners' insurance policies include hurricane deductibles, typically ranging from 2 percent to 5 percent of the home's value. If, for example, one's

TABLE 4.2. Homeowners' insurance claims

2008 status of homeowners' insurance claims
as a percentage of those filed.

	Full sample	MS	LA
Fully settled	77%	77%	78%
Partially settled	14	13	15
Pending	3	32	
Denied	4	6	3
Don't know/No answer	2	1	2
Total	100%	100%	100%
Total number of respondents	1816	597	1219

$150,000 home suffered severe damage from the storm, even with a cooperative adjuster and no controversy over the cause of the damage, the homeowner might be responsible for the first $3,000 to $7,500 of the cost of repairing the home. With so many affected residents experiencing severe financial problems, coming up with such high deductibles often proved quite difficult, if not impossible. As an important measure of recovery, we asked respondents about the status of their homeowners' insurance claims approximately three years after the storm. A summary of this information is provided in table 4.2. Findings are similar by state, with just over three-quarters of respondents having had their claims fully settled. This leaves almost a fourth with a partial settlement, a rejection, or a claim that was still pending.

Undoubtedly, those whose claims were rejected would experience stress and frustration. Also, based upon the context in which the question was asked, it is reasonable to assume that those who received only partial settlements were likely to be dissatisfied over that outcome. In addition, 4 percent of homeowners' claims were still pending in 2008. While that number may appear relatively small, it represents thousands of unfortunate homeowners whose claims were in limbo for at least three years after the storm.

An additional dimension of the insurance claims process involves the self-reported stress that homeowners experienced. To tap this dimension, respondents were asked to characterize the levels of stress stemming from working with homeowners' insurance companies. Table 4.3 reveals that stress levels were quite high. Varying little by state, significant majorities of the sample found these experiences to be at least "somewhat stressful," with almost a quarter indicating that they were "very stressful."

TABLE 4.3. Stress involved in insurance claims

How would you complete this sentence: After Katrina,
working with (homeowners' insurance) has been _____?

	Full sample	MS	LA
Very stressful	23%	22%	24%
Stressful	13	12	14
Somewhat stressful	26	26	27
No stress at all	36	38	34
Don't know/No answer	2	2	1
Total	100%	100%	100%
Total number of respondents	1816	597	1219

Even though Mississippi respondents reported being slightly less stressed by homeowners' insurance issues than did respondents in Louisiana, 60 percent reported some level of stress. These results clearly reveal an emergent post-Katrina stressor. As survivors attempted to secure funds to rebuild their homes, working with insurance companies created additional frustration and stress.

Although not reported in tabular form, additional breakdowns reveal racial disparities in the outcomes of homeowners' insurance claims. African American homeowners with property damage were slightly more likely than white homeowners to file claims (96 percent to 93 percent), but were significantly less likely to have their claims fully settled—while 82 percent of whites acknowledged fully settled claims, only 62 percent of African Americans fall into that category. African Americans were also twice as likely as whites to have partially settled homeowners' claims (25 percent versus 11 percent). Reactions to the experiences, however, appear to be relatively uniform. There were no significant differences in characterization of stress levels by race. Even so, it is important to note that insurance claims constitute yet another crucial concern where African American survivors fared worse than others.

FLOOD INSURANCE CLAIMS AND SETTLEMENTS

As noted above, the National Flood Insurance Program (NFIP) was designed to provide homeowner coverage for water damage that is excluded from basic homeowners' insurance policies. The program was established by Congress in 1968 as the number of private insurers refusing to insure homes in flood-prone areas reached crisis levels. The program is administered by private insurers, but is underwritten by the federal government. Such insurance is mandatory for those who carry federally insured mortgages on homes located in special flood hazard areas as designated by NFIP, although many private mortgage companies also require it.

Despite great potential for hurricane flooding, flood insurance coverage throughout Katrina's impact area was spotty at best. The Mississippi coast is home to large numbers of retirees who do not carry mortgages on their homes and were therefore not required to carry flood insurance. In Louisiana, many homes in flood-prone areas have been passed down through families and were not mortgaged. Without the mortgage requirement or the disposable income to pay for optional insurance, homeowners often lacked coverage. In addition, many of the homes that suffered extensive water damage were not insured because they were not in flood-prone areas. While we asked our respondents whether they had flood insurance and, if so, whether they filed a claim, we did not ask whether they would have filed a claim if they had had flood insurance. Thus, there is no sure way to determine the full extent to which this lack of coverage slowed down recovery

FIGURE 4.2. An example of the extensive flooding of residential neighborhoods in New Orleans, with a failed levee visible in the foreground, August 30, 2005. FEMA, photo by Jocelyn Augustine.

TABLE 4.4. Status of flood insurance claims

2008 status of flood insurance claims as a
percentage of those who filed.

	Full sample	*MS*	*LA*
Fully settled	87%	81%	88%
Partially settled	6	10	6
Pending	1	3	1
Denied	3	3	3
Don't know/No answer	2	2	2
Total	100%	100%	100%
Total number of respondents	623	91	532

after Katrina. Even so, our data suggest that the problems were severe and extensive. Among the subgroup of the sample whose homes were damaged, about half carried flood insurance. The numbers, however, varied significantly by state, with 21 percent in Mississippi and 63 percent in Louisiana reporting coverage. Among those who owned their homes at the time of the hurricane, experienced some amount of damage to their homes, and had flood insurance, 54 percent filed claims. This pattern varied little by state, with claims filed by 57 percent in Mississippi and 53 percent in Louisiana.

As another measure of recovery, it is important to look at the status of these claims at the time of the 2008 survey. A summary of this information is provided in table 4.4. Again, we find that a large majority (87 percent) of flood insurance claims had been fully settled, with percentages varying only slightly by state. Still, at least 10 percent endured what they must surely have considered to be less than adequate outcomes, with their claims either settled partially (6 percent), still pending (1 percent), or denied altogether (3 percent). Once again, while these percentages may appear relatively small, they represent thousands of homeowners who suffered unsatisfactory outcomes in their attempts to obtain settlements sufficient to rebuild their homes and their lives.

As with homeowners' insurance claims, those with flood insurance claims were asked to characterize their levels of stress in dealing with the insurance bureaucracy. Table 4.5 reveals that almost two-thirds of the sample reported experiencing some level of stress, with more than one in five responding that the experience was "very stressful." These data identify another issue in the host of emerging and ongoing stressors, which taken

TABLE 4.5. Stress involved in flood insurance claims

How would you complete this sentence: After Katrina,
working with (flood insurance) has been _____?

	Full sample	MS	LA
Very stressful	21%	22%	21%
Stressful	13	15	12
Somewhat stressful	23	24	23
No stress at all	31	33	42
Don't know/No answer	2	3	2
Total	100%	100%	100%
Total number of respondents	623	91	532

together over time create a context not at all conducive to post-disaster recovery.

Although not reported in tabular form, additional comparisons reveal state and racial disparities in the outcomes of flood insurance claims. While there were minimal racial differences in the percentages filing claims in Mississippi, that was not the case in Louisiana, where blacks were much more likely than whites to have filed a claim (72 percent vs. 48 percent). When it came to getting claims settled, blacks were about 20 percent less likely than whites to have their claims fully settled in Mississippi and about 10 percent less likely than whites to have their claims fully settled in Louisiana. While there were virtually no racial differences in stress levels from dealing with flood insurance in Louisiana, that was not the case in Mississippi, where blacks were 18 percent more likely than whites to report that the experience was either stressful or very stressful (37 percent for whites vs. 55 percent for blacks). Again, this racial disparity led to significantly more stress for African Americans in the impact area.

STATE GRANT PROGRAMS

In the year after Hurricane Katrina, the US Congress appropriated some $20 billion in emergency disaster relief and recovery aid in the form of Community Development Block Grants administered by the Department of Housing and Urban Development.[1] The majority of those funds were distributed to the states in the form of grants to help homeowners repair or rebuild their homes. Mississippi received $5.5 billion, while Louisiana received $13.4 billion. In Mississippi, the primary program created to distribute these monies was the Hurricane Katrina Homeowner Assistance Grant Program. Since the Mississippi Development Authority (MDA) administered the grants, they were often called MDA grants. In Louisiana, the grants were administered by a newly created entity called the Louisiana Road Home Program.

Participation in these programs caused considerable stress among Katrina survivors. While they were designed to help with recovery and were useful to a certain extent, the actual implementation of these grants was overly bureaucratized and unduly arduous. For those who went through the long and difficult application process only to be denied, the programs were worse than useless. Eligibility requirements were onerous and confusing, and numerous news media accounts highlighted significant obstacles to the effective use of the grant monies. In some cases, the grants provided only partial funding, with the expectation that homeowners would use other sources of funds to complete the job. Of course, many homeowners had no other sources of funds. In other cases, grant funds were not sufficient to cover the repairs for which they were initially allocated due to skyrocketing construction costs. Furthermore, some people were victimized during the rebuilding process, losing their grant funds to corrupt contractors and scam artists who demanded the money up front and never returned to perform the work.

According to initial guidelines formulated by the Department of Housing and Urban Development, states had considerable latitude in establishing eligibility requirements and other provisions of the grants.[2] As a result, specifications and outcomes in the implementation of these programs varied considerably between Mississippi and Louisiana. Accordingly, findings related to the two state grant programs are presented and discussed separately below.

MISSISSIPPI HOMEOWNER ASSISTANCE

The Mississippi Development Authority Homeowner Assistance Program[3] began accepting applications in April 2006. Awards were to be capped at $150,000, regardless of the actual amount of damage. While well over two hundred thousand housing units in Mississippi were damaged or destroyed, information from the MDA website indicates that only around forty thousand grant applications were processed. The first award checks were not issued until November 2006, more than a year after the storm. Overall, Mississippi authorities reported that about thirty thousand families actually received assistance from the program. Thus, only a small percentage of damaged housing units in Mississippi received grant funds to rebuild.

One of the greatest sources of stress in the MDA grants process was establishing eligibility. To be eligible, an applicant had to own a home in one of the following Mississippi counties: Harrison, Hancock, Jackson, or Pearl River. The applicant had to have occupied the home as a primary residence at the time of the storm and still own and occupy it at the time of the application. Perhaps most importantly, the home had to be outside the flood zone established by the National Flood Insurance Program prior to Katrina, but it had to have suffered flood damage during the storm. As if all this were not enough, the home had to have been insured with a basic homeowners' policy at the time of the storm, tragically guaranteeing that those who most needed help with rebuilding, the uninsured, were ineligible to receive grants. In addition to these narrow and inflexible requirements, obtaining the necessary documentation to establish eligibility was often problematic due to the loss and destruction of files, records, receipts, and other relevant documentation as a result of the storm.

In addition, use of the grant awards as an aid to overall recovery was constrained by further stringent provisions of the grants. The use of grant funds was limited to structural damage only; it could not be used for contents such as fixtures and appliances. Once rebuilt, the home had to meet strict code requirements and local ordinances, and had to be raised to whatever post-storm elevation FEMA recommended. Furthermore, the homeowner had to sign a covenant requiring that flood insurance be carried on the rebuilt residence in perpetuity.

Given these requirements, it is not surprising that among Mississippi homeowners who suffered damage to their homes, only 28 percent applied for an MDA grant. Also, as might be expected, completing an application was no guarantee of funding. As table 4.6 reveals, approximately three years after the storm, just over one-half of those who applied had received an award. One-fourth had been rejected and 15 percent were still pending. Given the level of damage sustained by these homes, such outcomes meant that many residents were forced into temporary housing for extended periods of time. Many others abandoned their homes altogether.

Although not reported in tabular form, additional breakdowns once again reveal racial disparity in the outcomes of MDA grant applications.

TABLE 4.6. MDA grant application outcomes

2008 status of Mississippi Development Authority grant applications as a percentage of those filed.	
Received an award	57%
Application still pending	15
Application rejected	24
Don't know/No answer	4
Total	100%
Total number of respondents	216

African Americans were significantly more likely than whites to apply for these funds (42 percent versus 26 percent), but were considerably less likely to receive an award (41 percent versus 62 percent). This pattern of racial exclusion further documents the race bias in recovery from Katrina.

LOUISIANA ROAD HOME PROGRAM

According to the Louisiana Road Home website, as of November 2018, the program had received almost 230,000 applications and provided compensation of slightly more than $9 billion to some 130,000 successful applicants;[4] thus, about 100,000 (44 percent) of those applying for Road Home grants were rejected. Like the MDA grants, compensation for damage from the storm was capped at $150,000. Eligibility requirements for Road Home grants were a bit simpler than those for the Mississippi program. Applicants had to have both owned and occupied the home at the time of the storm, and the home must have sustained at least $5,200 in damage. Unlike the Mississippi program, homes did not have to be outside a flood zone to be eligible. Also, those who did not have a homeowners' policy and flood insurance if the home was in a flood zone were not disqualified outright, as was the case in Mississippi, but they were penalized 30 percent of the total amount of the grant award, once again creating an additional hardship for those most in need.

Also, unlike their counterparts in Mississippi's MDA program, Louisiana recipients had greater latitude in spending the grant money. In some cases, they could receive grant funds even though they were exercising the option of selling their property to the state. However, if they did not sell their property to the state, they were required to occupy it as a primary residence within three years of receiving the grant funds. If the home was in a flood zone, they also had to sign a covenant requiring that flood insurance be carried on the home in perpetuity.

Given that the provisions in Louisiana's grant program were somewhat less onerous than those in Mississippi's, it is rather surprising that only a slightly higher percentage of Louisiana respondents applied for Road Home grants. According to our survey, just over one-third (35 percent) of those who suffered damage to their homes in Louisiana submitted grant applications. A summary of application status in 2008 is provided in table 4.7. Here we find that 62 percent received an award, about 21 percent were rejected, and 14 percent of Road Home applications were still pending some three years after the storm.

As with insurance claims, an additional dimension of the grants process involved the amount of stress experienced by homeowners. Almost two-thirds of those applying to the Road Home program found the experience to be at least "somewhat stressful." Less than one-third claimed that they experienced no stress at all. As was the case in Mississippi, what might have been a beneficial component of a timely recovery outcome turned into a traumatic bureaucratic nightmare. It should also be noted that many of those who did not apply for these grants were likely to have undergone similar emotional stress when, in the face of great need, they were intimidated by the onerous requirements and discouraged by the limited likelihood of success.

TABLE 4.7. Louisiana Road Home
grant application outcomes

2008 status of Louisiana Road Home grant applications as a percentage of those filed.	
Received an award	62%
Application still pending	14
Application rejected	21
Don't know/No answer	3
Total	100%
Total number of respondents	560

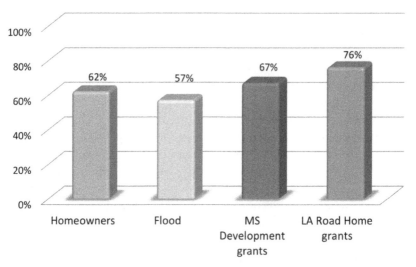

FIGURE 4.3. Stress related to seeking funds to rebuild (percent claiming "somewhat" stressful to "very" stressful).

SUMMARY

As noted in chapter 2, more than three-quarters of the 2008 respondents reported that Hurricane Katrina had caused their family financial problems, with one-fourth characterizing those problems as "severe." Most of the problems resulted from the extensive residential damage and destruction wreaked by the storm. For the vast majority of our respondents, the damage was so severe that they were unable to live in their homes after the storm. Thus, community recovery was heavily dependent on homeowners obtaining the necessary funding to repair and rebuild their primary residences. This need affected large percentages of the overall sample, with roughly three-fourths of respondents filing homeowners' insurance claims, one-fourth filing flood insurance claims, and almost one-third applying to their respective state grant programs. Unfortunately, the outcomes of these efforts were less than ideal.

The stress associated with the process of filing insurance claims and grant applications was an important social impediment to community recovery. In summarizing this stress, figure 4.3 shows that most respondents—usually by large majorities—experienced some amount of stress in dealing with these issues. The claims process for flood insurance was least stressful. At the same time, the Louisiana Road Home Program proved to be the most stress-inducing, with three-fourths of the sample reporting some level of stress associated with the pursuit of those grants. Of course, the Mississippi Development Authority grants were not far behind, with over two-thirds being stressed.

These results clearly reveal an important post-Katrina stressor. As survivors attempted to secure funds to rebuild their homes, working with insurance companies and state grant programs created additional hardship and aggravation. It is clear that obtaining needed resources for rebuilding was a major source of worry and frustration for applicants across the impact region. On this front, as with virtually all other findings, subgroup comparisons reveal racial disparities that consistently demonstrate the disadvantages experienced by African Americans both during the storm and in the process of recovery.

PHYSICAL HEALTH EFFECTS
OVERALL CHANGES AND LINGERING PROBLEMS

Although we survived Katrina, five years after the storm it seems like everyone in both my wife's extended family and mine are sick. Plus, family members who had health problems before Katrina are sicker than ever. Some say that they couldn't get to the doctor and couldn't get their meds for months after the storm. My blood pressure problem got worse and my lungs are still bothering me. My mother had a heart attack in the year after the storm and still suffers palpitations. My wife, who was a jogger and picture of perfect health before the storm, now battles asthma and headaches, and she can't exercise like she used to. We both worry about the health of our three children who complain of headaches, stomach problems, and fatigue. My youngest daughter can't participate in PE class due to "shortness of breath." The physicians said it was probably due to some sort of chemical exposure that she developed lung problems. After Katrina, our entire neighborhood was flooded with toxic water and our houses were full of mold dust. My in-laws developed COPD. My aunt got lung cancer and passed away last month. She smoked when she was young, but the cancer came soon after the storm. They tell me it's impossible to link all of these illnesses to Katrina, but I know that the soil in our yard is contaminated with toxic chemicals. I don't plant a spring garden anymore. I even wonder if I can get exposed cutting the grass. Such is life when you live with the toxic muck left by Katrina.

SURVIVOR FROM NEW ORLEANS

INTRODUCTION

When considering the most immediate and direct health consequences of a hurricane, the initial focus is on the injuries and deaths resulting from the

FIGURE 5.1. Unseen dangers are surely lurking in this massive Katrina debris pile near Pass Christian, Mississippi, January 3, 2006. FEMA, photo by Patsy Lynch.

winds and water of the storm. Of course, a major cause of death is drowning, which results from both the storm surge and from freshwater flooding due to excessive rain. Other direct effects include injuries and deaths resulting from flying debris and the structural collapse of homes and buildings. In addition to these direct effects, hurricanes pose numerous indirect threats to human life and health. These include car wrecks during evacuation, carbon monoxide poisoning from generators, heart attacks and strokes resulting from associated stress and strain, and electrocutions from downed power lines and poorly installed generators, just to name a few. Unfortunately, when it comes to any official accounting of morbidity and mortality associated with Katrina, records are woefully incomplete. Even the number of deaths is in dispute, although it surely approaches two thousand. For injuries, there is simply no reliable estimate.

Once a storm has passed, the dangers to survivors may actually intensify. In the case of Hurricane Katrina, the most disastrous post-storm danger was the levee failure and subsequent flooding of New Orleans, which resulted in thousands of people being trapped in their homes. As floodwaters continued to rise, many of those trapped sought shelter in their attics, only to be entombed with no escape route when waters rose over their roofs. But despite the violence of the storm and the horrors of its immediate aftermath, Hurricane Katrina caused more widespread consequences through long-term negative effects on the physical health and well-being of survivors. In this chapter, we review the numerous health threats associated with Katrina and its aftermath and provide an accounting of the perceived health effects as reported by our respondents.

POST-KATRINA ENVIRONMENTAL CONDITIONS

In assessing the health effects of Hurricane Katrina, we must recognize that the storm included major, devastating technological elements. In addition to the direct effects on people and the built environment, the storm disturbed and displaced massive amounts of hazardous material, leaving a toxic environment in its wake. To account for the "natural" and "technological" dimensions of disasters such as Katrina, researchers have combined these terms into the more appropriate descriptor, "natech disaster."[1] Disaster researchers generally concur that natech disasters are characterized by drastically prolonged periods of recovery, heightened levels of social conflict and community fragmentation, and serious negative consequences for the physical and mental health and overall well-being of survivors, all of which are evident in the aftermath of Katrina. We begin with the effect of Katrina on physical health conditions.

To gain a complete picture of the health consequences of Katrina, we must first consider the perilous environment in which survivors found themselves in the post-storm period. These perils can be categorized as follows: 1) exposure to mold and toxic materials; 2) presence of mountains of hazardous debris; 3) proliferation of insect and animal pests; 4) collapse of basic municipal infrastructure; 5) lack of food and potable water; 6) damaged and dangerous housing conditions; 7) shortages of health care facilities and providers; and 8) breakdown of domestic order. While one might reasonably expect such conditions to last for weeks and months after the storm, in the case of Katrina, these conditions persisted for years.

When Katrina's huge storm surge inundated the entire region and the subsequent levee failure flooded New Orleans, it created a "toxic soup" of household chemicals that were spilled during the storm (oil, gasoline, paints, solvents, cleaning agents, pesticides, herbicides, etc.). In addition, sewer systems were overwhelmed, resulting in the release of vast amounts of raw sewage containing dangerous levels of E. coli, fecal coliform bacteria, and other deadly pathogens. But this typical array of household chemicals and sewage was only a small part of the toxic soup. Other ingredients included vast amounts of similar substances from farms and businesses, as well as more hazardous materials from chemical plants, refineries, and

FIGURE 5.2. A recovery worker removes family photos from a mold-covered wall in New Orleans, October 23, 2005. FEMA, photo by Andrea Booher.

manufacturing plants. Even more ominous, according to a White House report, the overall area affected by Katrina was home to some 466 facilities handling large amounts of hazardous chemicals, as well as forty-seven toxic waste sites, which included sixteen Superfund sites.[2] These chemical releases were catastrophic and enduring in magnitude and scope for major parts of Louisiana and Mississippi.

In New Orleans, floodwaters from the failed levees mixed with the receding storm surge, mingling untold quantities of these hazardous materials and giving off fumes that fouled the air and burned the eyes. Some of the toxic pollution was obvious, as was the case with the Murphy Oil USA Refinery spill in a suburb just east of New Orleans that severely contaminated over eighteen hundred residences.[3] For the most part, however, the actual contents of the contaminated waters were not fully investigated, leaving significant ambiguity regarding levels of toxicity and the potential impact. And what happened to this toxic soup? Large amounts surged back into the Gulf or ran off into streams and rivers, but some settled into the soil, resulting in long-term contamination that will be virtually impossible to remove. In the New Orleans area, millions of gallons of this soup were pumped directly into Lake Pontchartrain, from which it would make its way into other waterways surrounding the city and ultimately into the Gulf of Mexico. The long-term impact of this contamination has been likened to a

FIGURE 5.3. A US Navy hospital corpsman tests for air contaminants emanating from the toxic sludge covering a residential street in St. Bernard Parish, Louisiana, September 12, 2005. US Navy, photo by Journalist First Class James Pinsky.

"toxic time bomb," with great uncertainty regarding the point at which the explosion will manifest itself, as well as the scope and severity of the damage it will wreak.

In addition to the toxic sludge, the receding storm surge and floodwaters left mountains of hazardous debris scattered across the impact area. The US Government Accounting Office reported that Hurricane Katrina generated more than one hundred million cubic yards of debris.[4] To get an idea of how much this is, note that one hundred million cubic yards of debris placed in a building with a floor measuring 100 × 100 feet would reach fifty-two miles into the sky. The more hazardous elements of the storm debris consisted primarily of the following: 1) hundreds of thousands of refrigerators and air conditioners leaking Freon; 2) vast quantities of electronic equipment such as computers, printers, TVs, stereos, etc., which contain significant amounts of lead, mercury, PCBs, and many other toxic materials; 3) hundreds of thousands of cars, trucks, motorcycles, boats, and recreational vehicles leaking oil, gas, anti-freeze, transmission fluid, battery acid, and power steering fluid; 4) countless decomposing corpses of drowned animals; and 5) huge amounts of spoiled and decaying food from destroyed homes, restaurants, markets, etc. Katrina's toxic attack is a classic case of massive nonpoint pollution. Chemicals from so many sources preclude a systematic accounting of the risks posed to the ecological areas and their human populations.

The debris itself created further hazards by providing shelter and breeding grounds for all manner of odious and dangerous pests. Insects, especially flies and mosquitos, proliferated in the decayed waste and standing water, raising concerns about insect-borne disease. Animal populations, including rats, mice, nutria, squirrels, and raccoons, were disturbed as they sought higher ground during the flooding. In addition to the potential for carrying disease, these vermin infested homes and businesses, chewing through wiring and causing structural damage. Furthermore, many of the household pets that had been left behind had to fend for themselves; these included not only cats and dogs but also snakes, scorpions, tarantulas, and other exotic creatures. Under such circumstances, both feral animals and stray pets can adopt aggressive and antagonistic behaviors, further contributing to the trauma and stress experienced by Katrina survivors.

In normal circumstances, local governments would be overwhelmed by such a massive amount of debris and its associated perils, but in the aftermath of Katrina, things were anything but normal. Municipal jurisdictions were utterly dysfunctional, and the basic infrastructure of municipal service delivery was shattered. Utility services were severely disrupted; water systems, natural gas, and the electric power grid were down throughout much of the affected area. Communications systems failed due to toppled telephone poles and wrecked cell phone towers. Roads were washed out or impassable due to damage and debris; bridges were washed away or in danger of collapse. Storm drainage and sewer systems were clogged; pumping stations were in ruins and treatment plants inoperable. In New Orleans, raw sewage was pumped directly into Lake Pontchartrain for weeks after the storm.

More than a terrible inconvenience, the lack of electricity resulted in numerous associated perils: carbon monoxide exposure from poorly placed and unventilated power generators, heat-related health problems due to the lack of air conditioning, and lack of refrigeration for various medicines, such as insulin, antibiotics, and vaccines. In addition, there were significant shortages of food and potable water resulting from the destruction of numerous wholesale and retail grocery and food service establishments. As a result of shortages, residents felt compelled to salvage food that was spoiled during the storm. This contributed to additional health risks such as salmonella, listeria, and E. coli. A lack of potable water meant dehydration risks, as well as the potential for waterborne illnesses from drinking contaminated water.

As detailed previously, hundreds of thousands of homes were rendered unfit for human habitation. Some were simply gone, while others were in danger of collapse. Many had been flooded by the storm surge and levee failure and were contaminated with various types of mold and bacteria. Spores released by mold and the airborne endotoxins given off by bacteria can cause numerous health problems, including lung inflammation and infections, skin rashes, allergic reactions, and asthma, as well as more serious diseases. In addition, older homes in many of the affected areas contained asbestos insulation, which is associated with an increased risk of cancer, as well as lead-based paints, which can cause a variety of serious health problems; post-Katrina conditions increased the risk of exposure to these materials. Given the extreme shortage of alternative accommodations, many survivors were forced to live for weeks or months in contaminated residential environments that posed significant health risks.

Due to the myriad perils left in the wake of Hurricane Katrina, the health care needs of survivors were both extensive and extreme. Once again, however, we find that available resources were grossly insufficient. This was due primarily to the destruction of health care facilities and the displacement of health care providers. Numerous hospitals, clinics, rehab centers, nursing homes, doctors' offices, and pharmacies were damaged or destroyed. For example, there were twenty-three hospitals with 3,679 beds operating in Orleans Parish before Katrina. After Katrina, there was one: the temporary USNS *Comfort*, a Mercy-class hospital ship with 270 beds.[5] As with the general population of residents, most health care providers were displaced by the storm, contributing to critical shortages of doctors, nurses, and allied health professionals. With no facilities in which to work, many did not return for weeks and months after the storm; some never returned.

Beyond a lack of basic health care facilities and providers, there was a shortage of drugstores, pharmacists, and medications. Both over-the-counter drugs and prescription medications were unavailable or inaccessible. These shortages affected not only those with Katrina-related health problems, but also those with preexisting conditions who were forced to deal with difficulties stemming from damaged or missing medical files, insurance information, and prescription records. Given that a relatively large proportion of the affected population suffered from chronic health problems such as diabetes, high blood pressure, heart failure, and kidney disease, all of which require regular maintenance medications, these circumstances constituted a physical health catastrophe. So how did these conditions affect the health of Hurricane Katrina survivors? We answer that question in the following section.

HEALTH CONSEQUENCES AS MEASURED IN OUR SURVEYS

The primary physical health effects of the storm on our respondents will be evaluated in terms of initial onset of Katrina-related health problems, as well as the increase in symptoms related to a variety of medical conditions occurring both during and after the storm. We collected information in five basic categories: 1) high blood pressure; 2) heart conditions; 3) respiratory problems; 4) headaches; and 5) stomach-related issues, including nausea. This information is combined with several general indicators of post-Katrina health measures to provide a description of changes in physical health and the onset of medical problems as experienced by survivors. Our analysis clearly reveals that Katrina produced serious illness throughout the target areas of Mississippi and Louisiana. And once again, it is clear that African Americans suffered disproportionately more negative health consequences than others.

One measure of the health effects of Katrina involves changes in respondents' overall state of health. To tap this dimension, we asked people whether their overall health had gotten better, stayed the same, or gotten

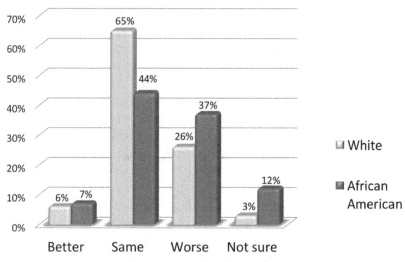

FIGURE 5.4. Changes in overall health since the storm, by race.

worse since the storm. In the full sample, only 7 percent indicated that their health had improved, while 29 percent stated that their health had gotten worse. When these results are broken down by race, as shown in figure 5.4, we find that African Americans were more likely than whites to state that their health had deteriorated. They were also much more likely to express uncertainty about the changes in their health.

We also addressed whether people believed that any decline in their health was hurricane-related by asking if they had "any health problems that you think might have resulted from or gotten worse due to your experience with the hurricane?" Overall, almost one in three respondents reported having developed health problems that they believed were related to their Katrina experiences. Given the extensive health-related dangers produced by the storm, this finding is not surprising. These results also vary considerably by race. As figure 5.5 reveals, African Americans were 13 percent more likely to have reported Katrina-related health problems than whites and, once again, were less certain about the health effects of the storm. This finding reinforces the conclusion that African Americans suffered more damage across all dimensions of Katrina impacts, including health.

To discover what types of health issues Katrina survivors faced, we asked them to identify the sorts of health problems that had either developed or gotten worse after the storm. We asked specifically about headaches, stomach issues, heart rhythm, hypertension, and respiratory problems. As revealed in figure 5.6, there were significant increases in every category of health problems, with the greatest increases occurring in the prevalence of respiratory disorders, not surprising given the levels of toxic exposure.

Another important measure involves Katrina's impact on people already dealing with health problems prior to the storm. If we focus solely on those individuals with preexisting conditions, we find that the burdens of Katrina fall quite heavily on them. As shown in figure 5.7, among those who had some sort of respiratory issue before Katrina, over 60 percent stated that their condition worsened after the storm. In addition, headaches, heart problems, stomach disorders, and hypertension all were reported to have become worse after Katrina.

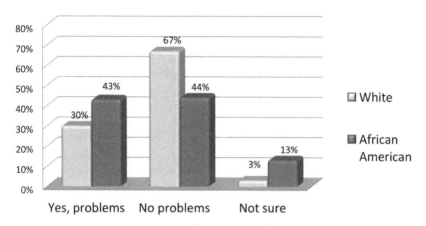

FIGURE 5.5. Katrina-related health problems, by race.

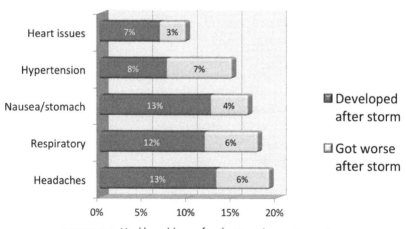

FIGURE 5.6. Health problems after the storm (percent reporting problems that developed or got worse after the storm).

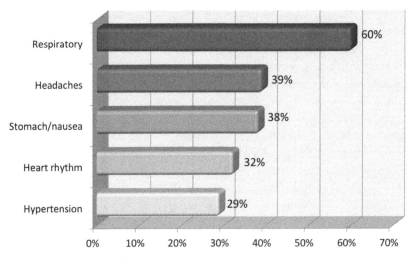

FIGURE 5.7. Types of health problems among those with pre-existing conditions (percent reporting that the problem got worse after the storm).

These data somewhat understate the prevalence of these health issues because they do not take into account the unfortunate fact that some Katrina survivors experienced problems across more than one category. Aggregating these issues across categories reveals that 38 percent of the overall sample experienced at least one health problem that had either started at the time of Katrina or gotten worse after the storm. More than one in five respondents experienced more than one problem. As a proportion of those who reported at least one problem, 43 percent experienced only one, while 25 percent experienced two problems, and another 33 percent experienced more than two. Clearly, Hurricane Katrina had a variety of significant negative health effects on many of its victims.

Given the predominance of respiratory problems, as well as headaches and stomach issues, among survivors, we investigated whether responses regarding health might be related to exposure to hazardous substances that were released into the environment. The most troublesome and ubiquitous threats involved exposure to toxic chemicals and mold. The ultimate impact of these threats varies considerably depending on the type of chemical and extent of exposure. Five of the more dangerous chemicals found in testing after the storm included lead, mercury, thallium, cadmium, chromium, and arsenic.[6] These chemicals were found in quantities that were unlikely to cause immediate acute toxicity. However, chronic exposure to even small amounts of these chemicals is associated with cancer, brain damage, and birth defects. Much more common was exposure to the ubiquitous mold growing in storm-flooded areas. Even short-term mold exposure can cause respiratory distress, including coughing, runny nose, congestion, and headaches.

For those with preexisting health conditions, toxic exposure can have very serious consequences such as aggravating asthma and other allergic reactions, or causing breathing problems, infections, and other pulmonary disorders. In addition, the mycotoxins produced by certain types of mold common in flooded and abandoned structures can have severe long-term health consequences, including organ damage.

While our survey findings do not address specifics related to these longer-term health consequences, we did ask respondents for their perceptions of such exposure and its potential impact. Of course, when it comes to reports of both health issues and environmental exposure, these data reflect respondents' perceptions rather than any objective measurement. However, the results do provide important evidence of a correlation between these variables. As shown in figure 5.8, those who believe their families were exposed to dangerous chemicals were three times more likely to report that their health had gotten worse since the storm, and they were almost three times more likely to believe that their health problems were a consequence of their Katrina experiences. Undoubtedly, toxic exposure and its potential long-term impact on health will continue to serve as a source of stress and anxiety for Katrina survivors.

When it comes to health-related sources of stress and anxiety, two addi-

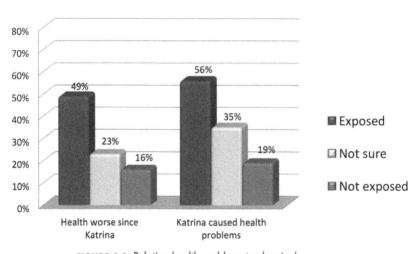

FIGURE 5.8. Relating health problems to chemical exposure.

tional issues of consequence remain. One is the formaldehyde exposure associated with FEMA trailers that was discussed in chapter 3. To determine the impact of FEMA trailers on perceptions of toxic exposure, we compare those who lived in trailers with those who did not. Here we find that 57 percent of those who lived in FEMA trailers believed they or their family members had been exposed to dangerous chemicals, compared to 33 percent of those who had not lived in the trailers.

While we did not address it in the survey, it might also be noted that another major area of toxic exposure involved the use of contaminated construction materials in the process of residential reconstruction. In the affected area, as many as one hundred thousand homes were rebuilt, repaired, or remodeled using Chinese drywall containing toxic amounts of sulfur. Fumes given off by the drywall caused serious health problems, including nausea, headaches, digestive ailments, asthma, and other respiratory conditions. In addition, the toxic vapors corroded wiring and copper tubing throughout the homes, causing severe damage to the electrical grid and plumbing systems as well as air conditioners, appliances, and electronics. Many families who had finally returned to their homes after months of displacement from Katrina were once again forced to leave due to these recurrent exposures and health issues. Clearly, formaldehyde and Chinese drywall, added to all the other health threats present, can be expected to negatively affect the physical well-being of Katrina survivors well into the future.

CHANGES IN HEALTH PERCEPTION FROM 2008 TO 2010

As can be seen in figure 5.9, between 2008 and 2010, there was no change in the proportion of people who reported Katrina-related health problems. In each case, approximately three in ten respondents reported such problems. The only difference was that many of those who were unsure about their health in 2008 had decided that they did not have Katrina-related problems by 2010. The finding that people were more confident about the health effects of Katrina is encouraging in the sense that it should allow, at least for some, a decrease in anxiety regarding long-term prognoses. While this is a positive finding, it may be somewhat misplaced since, in actuality, long-term negative health effects may not manifest themselves until decades after the storm.

The 142 respondents who reported continued Katrina-related health issues in 2010 were also asked about the types of problems they were ex-

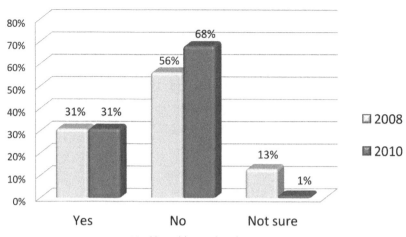

FIGURE 5.9. Health problems related to Katrina experience (comparison of 2008 and 2010 results).

periencing and whether or not they had received a diagnosis from a medical professional. At that time, the most common categories of problems were high blood pressure and headaches, unlike the 2008 findings, in which the most commonly reported problem involved respiratory issues. In addition, large majorities stated that their health problems had been confirmed by medical diagnosis, providing some confirmation that these self-reports were relatively accurate.

CONCLUSION

The physical health effects resulting from Hurricane Katrina are genuinely shocking. This is especially the case when considering that our sample of just over twenty-five hundred respondents represents millions of people throughout the impact area. While it is common to think of the legacy of a hurricane in terms of wind speeds, storm surges, and infrastructure damage, one of Katrina's primary legacies is the significant negative effects on the physical well-being of survivors. These physical health effects also have consequences for the mental and behavioral well-being of the population. The suffering and uncertainty associated with poor physical health contribute significantly to anxiety, depression, and stress. This is especially the case when considering the potential long-term impacts of toxic exposure. We next turn our attention toward these mental health consequences.

MENTAL HEALTH EFFECTS
LINGERING PATTERNS OF DEPRESSION AND PTSD

Katrina is not over! It's been more than two years since the storm destroyed our home in New Orleans East and my family, relatives, and neighbors still suffer flashbacks that bring back feelings of depression and sometimes panic attacks. Driving around my old neighborhood, I see homes that have not been rebuilt and probably never will be. The abandoned theme park out on I-10 is another distressing reminder. Many of our relatives have moved out of the area, but still talk about how their lives were ruined because of the storm. Lost jobs and financial problems have led to divorces, heavy drinking, and drugs for a lot of people. My cousins avoid family gatherings because talk will eventually include Katrina, causing resentment and anger, then arguments and crying. I have been divorced for five years and can't get away from the pain. As I said at the beginning of this interview, Katrina is not over, and for me, it never will be.

SURVIVOR FROM NEW ORLEANS EAST

INTRODUCTION

Perhaps the most pervasive and lasting human effects of Hurricane Katrina are the mental and behavioral health problems associated with the storm experience and its aftermath. Although a few residents of the affected area did not suffer a significant personal loss, practically everyone knew family members, neighbors, friends, or coworkers who were, in one way or another, casualties of Katrina. The psychological and emotional trauma of the human suffering was compounded by the hurricane's devastation of the built environment. The destruction of homes carried with it the loss

FIGURE 6.1. A Katrina survivor evacuated to the Houston Astrodome is comforted by a Red Cross worker. Houston, Texas, September 2, 2005. FEMA, photo by Andrea Booher.

of family heirlooms and photographs, documents and records, furniture and appliances, indeed, all the necessities of everyday life. The destruction of business and commercial properties meant the loss of livelihoods for business owners and their workers. Even the lucky few whose homes and businesses escaped damage were confronted with the devastation of community infrastructure and the shredding of the social fabric of their city or town. Virtually no one caught in the path of the storm was immune from the consequences of Katrina.

In the weeks and months after the storm, survivors had no choice but to bury their dead, bind their wounds, and obtain shelter from the elements, but their emotional and psychological needs were often ignored. Evidence of this neglect can be found in a number of studies undertaken in the wake of Katrina. For example, a survey by the Centers for Disease Control and Prevention conducted seven weeks after the storm in Jefferson and Orleans Parishes found that in more than one in four households, there was at least one person in need of psychological counseling, but in less than 2 percent of households had anyone actually received counseling services.[1] One might expect this low number in the immediate post-storm environment, but inadequate counseling was an ongoing problem. Another survey, conducted six months after the storm, revealed that while 31 percent of survivors exhibited symptoms of a psychological disorder, only about 10 percent had received treatment.[2] The stigma associated with seeking mental health services undoubtedly contributed to this situation, but there were a number of other causes.

A major factor resulting in the lack of appropriate attention to mental and behavioral health problems involved the diminished capacity of the health care system to deliver such services. The storm itself caused extensive destruction of the health care delivery infrastructure, with the overwhelming majority of hospitals and clinics throughout the impact area closed due to storm damage. In addition, mental health professionals and support staff were scattered to the winds, many never to return. For example, in the weeks after the storm, only about 10 percent of New Orleans's roughly two hundred psychiatrists were practicing in the area.[3] On April 23, 2007, a *Times-Picayune* article summed it up: "Mental patients have nowhere to go."[4] Another issue was that many people failed to address or even acknowledge their own mental health problems because there were simply too many other issues demanding attention. In the short run, food, shelter, and physical injuries and ailments were understandably considered more pressing than feelings of anxiety or depression. In the longer term, rebuilding, relocation, and reemployment might take precedence over concerns for psychological well-being. Indeed, many people likely believed that with full physical recovery from the storm, mental and behavioral problems would resolve themselves. Unfortunately, large numbers of Katrina survivors have never achieved full recovery, with many continuing to suffer from lingering psychological trauma.

In this chapter, we review the various sources of stress experienced by Katrina survivors, with emphasis on those stressors included in our survey data. We then present our findings on the mental health status of survivors, focusing primarily on two important pathologies: depression and post-traumatic stress disorder (PTSD). Then we explore the relationship between traumatic hurricane experiences and measures of mental and behavioral health in the population. In addition, we review the significant racial disparities evident in our findings, and end with comparisons of 2008 survey results and those from the 2010 follow-up survey.

SOURCES OF PSYCHOLOGICAL STRESS AND TRAUMA

In measuring the mental and behavioral effects of Katrina, it is important to review the various sources of anxiety and stress. Potential stressors measured in our 2008 survey are summarized in table 6.1, in which the focus

TABLE 6.1. Hurricane-related stressors (negative experiences as percentage of full sample)

Residential damage minor or more	96%
Reported at least some financial problem	76
Had more than $10,000 in total losses	71
Displaced from home	61
Experienced family separation	59
Experienced stress w/homeowners' insurance	45
Spent more than $10,000 just on home repair	43
Believed exposed to toxic materials	25
Worried toxins still in neighborhood	22
Experienced stress w/grants	22
Lived in FEMA trailer	18
Experienced stress w/flood insurance	14
Experienced stress w/litigation	4

is placed on the negative outcome. As can be seen in this table, substantial percentages of storm survivors reported highly stressful experiences related to Katrina. When assessing the potential consequences of such stressors, it is important to keep in mind their cumulative impact. Many of those surveyed experienced several of these stressors, and some experienced virtually all of them.

One stressor not reported in this table is the initial storm experience. Recall from chapter 2 that our survey respondents reported either evacuating their homes (79 percent) or sheltering in place (19 percent). Among those sheltering in place, about one-half (10 percent of the entire sample) were rescued during the storm. Of course, these storm experiences were major stressors for all Katrina survivors, but assigning relative levels of stress to these categories is not possible due to the wide variation in individuals' characteristics and responses, such as financial circumstances, family situations, health conditions, etc. In addition, even where survivors shared similar characteristics, one can only speculate about relative levels of stress resulting from sheltering in place versus evacuating. For example, it would be tempting to suggest that having to be rescued during the hurricane might be the most stressful storm experience, but one might well experience a higher level of stress if there is a need for rescue and no rescue is forthcoming. On the one hand, even without the need for rescue, sheltering in place had to be extremely stressful as the storm approached, with weather conditions deteriorating and forecasts becoming progressively more perilous.

This foreboding would be compounded by second-guessing the initial decision to stay, which would naturally come with the rain pounding, the wind howling, and debris smashing against the sides of one's house.

On the other hand, the decision to evacuate obviously involved a great deal of uncertainty and anxiety as well. One would face questions regarding when to leave and what to take, which direction to go, what the traffic would be like, whether gasoline would be available along the way, where shelter might be found, and how long it would take to get there. As if that were not enough, there would also be worry about those who had been left behind, how long it might be before one could return home, and to what sorts of conditions one would be returning. Based upon these realities, virtually everyone in Katrina's path experienced some degree of psychological stress and trauma associated with their initial storm experience.

Once the storm was over and conditions allowed for a return home, stress levels might actually go from bad to worse. While the anticipation of returning to the storm-ravaged area would be a nagging worry, beholding the actual destruction would be traumatizing for many survivors. How would it feel to see an empty concrete slab where a family home full of memories and mementos had been?

Before reviewing evidence of the psychological impacts of these experiences, we must further acknowledge other potential sources of stress for Katrina survivors that were not addressed in our surveys.[5] Some of the most severe included the death or serious injury of family members, friends, neighbors, fellow church members, and coworkers. Also, while we asked about damage to one's home, we did not ask about loss or damage to cars, boats, or recreational vehicles. Nor did we ask about the post-Katrina condition of places of worship or places of employment. Regarding employment, while we asked about current employment status, we did not collect data on potential periods of unemployment or underemployment after Katrina, nor on changes in career expectations for individuals or their children. All of these factors would have a major impact on the stress levels experienced by Katrina survivors. However, while specific measures of such stress are missing, we believe that overall stress levels are likely to be reflected in the items we did measure. In other words, a respondent will evaluate the stress associated with damage to their homes, for example, in the context of their overall stress levels stemming from the sum of their Katrina experiences. As one might expect, the consequences of this stress include significant psychological symptoms as reported by survivors.

It is a truism to note that exposure to disaster-related stress will have consequences for the mental and behavioral health of survivors, especially in the areas of depression and post-traumatic stress disorder. There is a massive literature that supports this contention. One of the objectives of this study is to explore the relationship between storm experiences and these negative mental health outcomes. To accomplish this, respondents were asked a number of questions to assess their mental health status. We will present these findings and then relate them to a selected group of the stressors discussed above.

To measure the emotional and psychological consequences of Katrina, we relied on two multi-item scales. For depression, we used the Center for Epidemiological Studies Depression Scale (CES-D). For post-traumatic stress disorder, we used the Intrusive Recollections component of the Impact of Events Scale. The CES-D scale is a somewhat crude but nevertheless reliable measure of depression that has been validated in numerous psychological and sociological studies.[6] It consists of a series of questions that measure how often individuals experience negative feelings that are commonly associated with depression. Individuals were asked, "On how many days during the past week have you had the following experiences or feelings . . . ?" The specific questions, with summary results, are presented in table 6.2.

Here we see that two years after the storm, relatively large proportions of the sample reported experiencing some depression-related feelings. While not evident in this presentation, many of these respondents reported having experienced multiple symptoms on multiple days. For example, on most of the measures some 8 percent to 10 percent of respondents reported having such feelings on all seven days in the past week, and 15 percent reported having sleep problems on all seven days.

To get a more complete picture of depression among Katrina survivors, these data can be aggregated to obtain individual scores according to a formula commonly used in previous research studies of depression.[7] This formula translates the number of days experiencing each symptom aggregated across the full range of symptoms to obtain a score that can be used to determine whether a patient is at risk for depression. Results for the full sample are presented in figure 6.2.

This figure reveals that one out of four respondents reported sufficient symptomatology to be considered at risk for depression. To explore the consequences of depression for Katrina survivors, we can compare their symp-

TABLE 6.2. Symptoms of depression (percentage of people experiencing this symptom of depression on at least one of the last seven days)

I had trouble falling asleep or staying asleep	42%
I felt sad	42
I felt that I could not get going	39
I had trouble keeping my mind on what I was doing	38
Everything that I did took a great effort	38
I was bothered by things that usually do not irritate me	36
I felt that I could not get rid of the blues	33
I felt lonely	28
I lost my appetite	20
I felt that my life was a failure	14

n=2548

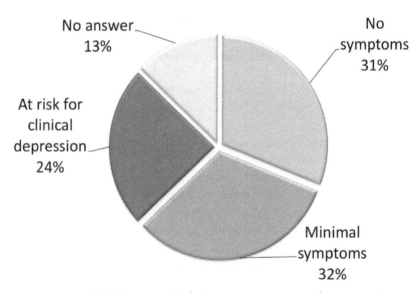

FIGURE 6.2. CES-D Depression Scale (aggregate scores reported in categories).

toms to responses on another question. One of the potential consequences involves feelings of powerlessness. To measure this, we asked respondents to agree or disagree with the following statement: "Since Katrina, I don't feel I have the power to make important decisions in my life." Among those at risk for clinical depression, 42 percent agreed with the statement, while only 4 percent of those exhibiting no symptoms agreed. This finding provides confirmation of the validity of our depression measure. It also represents a limited but compelling bit of evidence of Katrina's significant negative consequences for the mental health of survivors. Such consequences are especially problematic considering the scarcity of mental health care resources available to diagnose and treat depression in the affected area, a condition that prevailed for years after the storm.

Our PTSD measure, the Intrusive Recollections component of the Impact of Events Scale, consists of a series of questions regarding the psychological effects of a traumatic experience. Its use has been extensively assessed in previous research and found to be valid and reliable.[8] For our surveys, the standard questions were tailored to reference respondents' experiences with Katrina. The lead-in to the series is phrased as follows: "The next few questions deal with the impact of a stressful life event. For each question, think only about Hurricane Katrina and tell me whether the experiences have occurred not at all, rarely, sometimes, or often." The specific questions, with summary results, are presented in table 6.3.

With up to three-fourths of the sample reporting at least some symptom of PTSD, it appears that PTSD may be a more prevalent problem for Katrina survivors than depression. However, we acknowledge that these are rather crude measures for assessing the mental health impacts of the storm. Fortunately, as with depression, these data can be scored and summarized in the aggregate.[9] The resulting scores are used to identify the incidence of PTSD symptoms ranging from subclinical to severe, as shown in figure 6.3.

TABLE 6.3. Symptoms of post-traumatic stress disorder (percentage of people having experienced this symptom of PTSD)

Other things kept making me think about Hurricane Katrina	75%
I thought about Hurricane Katrina when I didn't want to	71
Pictures of Hurricane Katrina popped into my mind	69
Any reminder brought back feelings about Hurricane Katrina	64
I had waves of strong feelings about Hurricane Katrina	60
I was watchful and on guard	50
I felt irritable and angry because of Hurricane Katrina	46
I had trouble falling asleep or staying asleep	43
I was jumpy and easily startled	29
I had dreams about Hurricane Katrina	25
Reminders of Katrina caused me to have physical reactions	22

n=2548

These findings confirm the previous suggestion that PTSD was an even more common problem for Katrina survivors than depression. Over two-thirds of the sample experienced clinical symptoms of PTSD and, for more than one in five, those symptoms put them in the severe range. Undoubtedly, many survivors did not recognize these emotional experiences as symptoms of PTSD. Even if they had, as noted above, the opportunities to obtain treatment were certainly minimal.

While we are limited in our ability to directly connect PTSD with behavior, we do have one question that provides insight into the manner in which these symptoms affected the lives of survivors. We asked respondents to either agree or disagree with this statement: "Since Hurricane Katrina, there have been more arguments in my family." These results are very telling—a full 49 percent of those in the severe range for PTSD symptoms agreed that there were more arguments in the family, while only 8 percent of those in the subclinical range agreed. In addition to irritability, PTSD is highly associated with substance misuse, domestic violence, and suicide. Thus, PTSD is certainly one of the most significant negative consequences of Katrina, and yet it received scant attention from public health workers and emergency management officials in the follow-up to the storm.

Overall, these findings paint a picture of a region where close to half of the population exhibits some symptoms of depression and over two-thirds

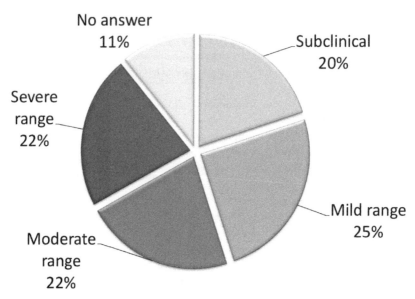

FIGURE 6.3. Impact of Events Scale (aggregate scores reported in categories).

TABLE 6.4. Hurricane stressors and mental health effects

	Displaced from home		Separated from family		Financial problems		Hazardous exposure	
	Yes	No	Yes	No	Yes	No	Yes	No
PTSD severe	31%	15%	32%	16%	51%	9%	42%	13%
Depression at risk	34%	19%	34%	20%	57%	9%	47%	15%

show signs of PTSD. But to what extent can these negative mental health findings be directly attributed to hurricane experiences? While there are many quantitative techniques that can be used to answer this question, sophisticated statistical analysis is beyond the scope of this book. For our purposes, we will compare the scores on depression and PTSD with four hurricane-related stressors: whether respondents had to move out of their homes after the storm; whether they were separated from family members because of the storm; whether the storm caused severe financial problems; and whether they believed they had been exposed to hazardous chemicals. These results are presented in table 6.4.

In every case, those having experienced hurricane stressors were significantly more likely to have reported PTSD and depression symptoms. In most cases, they were two to three times more likely to suffer these mental health problems than those who did not experience the stressors. The most extreme example involves family finances. Those reporting severe financial problems were almost five times more likely to suffer from PTSD and almost six times more likely to be depressed. These comparisons provide compelling evidence of the negative mental health effects of Katrina. It is important also to note that these findings do not account for the cumulative effects of these experiences on Katrina survivors. Many of our respondents may have few or no symptoms of either condition, while others may be clinically depressed as well as exhibiting severe symptoms of PTSD.

RACIAL DISPARITIES IN MENTAL HEALTH EFFECTS

We have seen in previous chapters that on many of our measures, African Americans suffered more negative consequences from the storm than whites. It might then be expected that they would also exhibit more mental

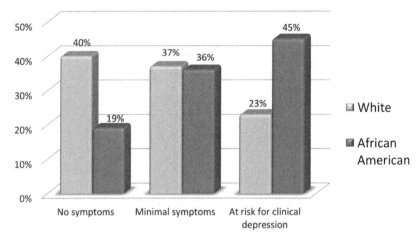

FIGURE 6.4. Racial disparities in symptoms of depression (as reflected in CES-D scores).

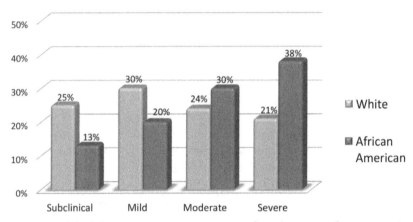

FIGURE 6.5. Racial disparities in PTSD symptoms (as reflected in Impact of Events scores).

health symptoms. Indeed, this is the case. As shown in figure 6.4, African Americans are almost twice as likely as whites to be at risk for clinical depression. Likewise, figure 6.5 reveals that they are significantly more likely to exhibit symptoms of PTSD.

As mentioned above, some of these differences are the result of the heavier burdens African Americans endured in the areas of financial loss, family separation, residential displacement, etc. Among other factors, racial disparities in health care prior to the storm also played a role. Due at least in part to their lower socioeconomic status, African Americans are more likely in general to suffer from poor health, especially in the prevalence of chronic diseases. These conditions made it more difficult for them to endure the storm and were often made significantly worse by the storm experience. After the storm, conditions for African Americans continued to worsen due to limited access to care, lack of health insurance, and low health literacy. But regardless of the causes, the racial disparities in the consequences of disasters demonstrate that emergency management officials and the health care system at large have failed some of the most vulnerable members of those communities caught in the path of Katrina.

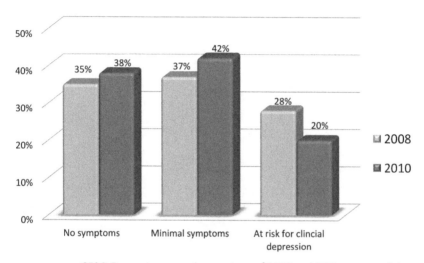

FIGURE 6.6. CES-D Depression scores (comparisons of 2008 and 2010 survey results).

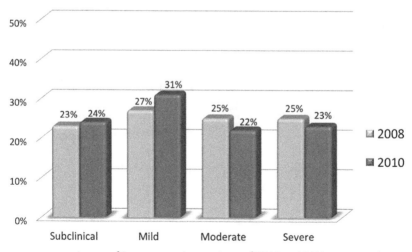

FIGURE 6.7. Impact of Events scores (comparisons of 2008 and 2010 survey results).

FIGURE 6.8. A scene from the Superdome, August 28, 2005. In the early hours of sheltering there, victims could not have guessed at the coming nightmare that would haunt many of them indefinitely. FEMA, photo by Marty Bahamonde.

Both the Impact of Events Scale and the CES-D Scale were repeated in the follow-up survey conducted in 2010. One might assume that five years after the storm, survivors would have experienced a return to normalcy that included a lessening of these PTSD and depression symptoms. To see if that assumption is warranted, we present comparisons of these two measures in figures 6.6 and 6.7.[10]

The most striking thing about these comparisons is how little things changed between three and five years after the storm. Obviously, the overall slow pace of recovery, as reported in previous chapters, has tended to prolong the prevalence of mental health problems. In addition, the lack of access to health care resources and providers, which is typically a greater problem in mental health than in physical health, has played an unfortunate role.

Based upon our findings, it is evident that large numbers of Katrina survivors have been dealing with debilitating symptoms of PTSD and depression. We have shown that these disorders can be connected directly with Katrina-related experiences and outcomes. Although social scientists are careful not to assume causation when interpreting such comparisons, given the context of the survey and our understanding of the human effects of disasters, there is little doubt that the storm, along with the inept response and recovery efforts, caused survivors intense stress, which in turn resulted in serious mental and behavioral health problems. In the absence of the mental health resources and providers needed to appropriately diagnose and deliver treatment for these conditions, the negative consequences continued to affect individuals, families, and communities for many years after the storm. Clearly this is an area where significant progress is needed so that the trauma and torment of Katrina are not repeated as a consequence of future hurricanes.

SUMMING UP AND LESSONS LEARNED

My life in New Orleans is over for the time being—
I have to start over completely.

NEW ORLEANS RESIDENT WINDI SEBREN, SEPTEMBER 2005

I can only imagine that this is what Hiroshima
looked like sixty years ago.

MISSISSIPPI GOVERNOR HALEY BARBOUR, AUGUST 2005

Hurricane Katrina, the "Storm of the Century," destroyed the built and modified environments across a large swath of the northern Gulf Coast and, most importantly, changed the lives of millions of people caught in its path. Over eighteen hundred individuals died, as many as two million were uprooted from their homes, families were separated for extended periods of time, and in the storm's aftermath a series of financial and bureaucratic nightmares haunted survivors, causing prolonged stress and anxiety, and resulting in depression and PTSD that would last for years. In addition, the potential health effects caused by exposure to vast amounts of hazardous materials and poisonous chemicals spilled during the storm will continue as a source of stress and anxiety for storm survivors into the foreseeable future.[1]

While there have been countless works chronicling the characteristics and consequences of Katrina, this book provides a unique presentation of original data collected from survivors who were directly in the path of the storm. As reported here, the experiences and perceptions of people in affected communities reveal a horror story that staggers the imagination. Before turning to a general summary of these findings, we will review a final survey measure of Katrina's consequences: survivors' expectations for the recovery of their communities. We end the chapter, and the book, with

FIGURE 7.1. In this September 6, 2005, photo taken after the storm, destruction in Long Beach, Mississippi, looks like it could have been the result of a nuclear bomb. FEMA, photo by Mark Wolfe.

practical suggestions for applying lessons learned from our research as supported by related academic literature.

EXPECTATIONS FOR RECOVERY

As table 7.1 reveals, in 2008, most residents believed community recovery would take a long time, projecting full recovery, if it happened at all, well into the future. For a majority of our 2008 respondents, community recovery was expected to take at least five more years, which would then be eight years after the storm. More than one in five believed recovery would take at least ten years, with almost 8 percent of those feeling that their communities "will never fully recover" from Katrina's devastation. In addition, a relatively large number (13 percent) were unable to offer an opinion on this issue, likely reflecting rather pessimistic attitudes.

We also addressed the topic of recovery in our 2010 follow-up survey. When asked about the then current status of recovery, a full three-fourths of the sample acknowledged that their communities had yet to recover. The results also revealed a degree of ongoing pessimism, with 14 percent saying their communities were making little progress toward recovery and another 10 percent saying that the community "will probably never recover."

One of the drivers of these negative attitudes involved an intervening event. In the spring of 2010, a couple of months prior to our second survey, the largest oil spill in North American history flooded the Gulf of Mexico with over two hundred million gallons of oil. Regrettably, there was major overlap between the areas damaged by the spill and the impact area of Katrina. Once again, residents faced a disaster of enormous proportions, further challenging their well-being and resiliency. The additional oil spill–related stress, trauma, and disruption certainly slowed the process of recovery from Katrina. This was confirmed by respondents in the follow-up survey, a full 76 percent of whom said that the oil spill would negatively impact recovery from the storm.

Based upon subsequent developments, it would appear that our respondents were realistically pessimistic about the recovery process. As of this writing, fourteen years after Katrina, there are still many visible reminders of the storm. To the east of New Orleans, the Six Flags Amusement Park stands deserted, a ghost-like memorial to Katrina's devastation. As one enters the city from the east on Interstate 10, numerous abandoned homes and commercial establishments are evident, and blue tarps still dot the landscape of roofs visible from the elevated highway. Driving along the Mississippi Gulf Coast, one sees that the once-bustling communities of

TABLE 7.1. 2008 expectations for community recovery

Tell me how long you believe it will be before your community is completely recovered from the impact of Hurricane Katrina?

	Full sample	MS	LA
Already recovered	9%	6%	11%
1 to 2 years	9	7	11
3 to 5 years	16	16	15
6 to 10 years	26	30	24
More than 10 years	14	18	12
Will never fully recover	8	8	7
Don't know/No answer	18	15	20
Total	100%	100%	100%
Total number of respondents	2548	810	1738

FIGURE 7.2. An aerial photo of Six Flags Amusement Park taken two weeks after the storm, on September 14, 2005. The park, though still there, remains abandoned. FEMA, photo by Bob McMillan.

Waveland, Bay St. Louis, and Pass Christian are virtually gone, with large stretches of land devoid of homes, stores, and shops.

These effects were so disturbing and disruptive that for years after the storm many residents continued to leave their communities without any intention of returning. In a certain sense, many of the pre-Katrina communities are now invisible, locked only in the memories of former residents, and in time such memories will have vanished forever.

SUMMARY OF FINDINGS

Documenting the consequences of Hurricane Katrina is a complicated process. One must take into account the context in which the hurricane occurred; the actual storm experiences of survivors, which might include evacuating or sheltering in place; and the trauma of witnessing post-storm devastation, as well as dealing with the dangers posed by mold, hazardous materials, storm debris, pest infestations, etc. Furthermore, the frustration and aggravation suffered by Katrina survivors in dealing with an intransigent, unsympathetic, and overly bureaucratized response from both gov-

Psychological health		Physiological health	Sociological effects	Economic effects	
Mental health	**Behavioral health**	• Headaches • Fatigue • Dizziness • Nausea • Vomiting • Respiratory distress • Cardiovascular disorders • Eye problems • Dermatitis • Hypertension • Human toxicity • Central nervous system disorders • Increased cancer risk	• Decline in social capital • Increased social conflict (deviance, intolerance, insularity) • Corrosion associated with short-term influx of outsiders • Population displacement • Reduced trust in others (both fellow community members and gov't officials) • Loss of community identity	**Primary individual effects**	**Primary community effects**
• Anxiety • Depression • PTSD • Suicide ideation	• Substance abuse • Self-isolation • Somatic complaints • Domestic abuse • Criminality • Suicide			• Income loss • Job loss • Depletion of savings • Property damage (homes, waterfront, boats) • Increased costs (health care, gas, seafood)	• Reduced tax revenue • Market impairment (declines in demand for business activity and tourism) • Brand damage

FIGURE 7.3. Hurricanes: Array of potential human effects.

ernmental officials and the insurance industry cannot be overstated. The negative consequences of these experiences constitute an astounding array of physical, psychological, social, and economic effects. These unfortunate consequences are categorized and summarized in figure 7.3.

The realities of these human effects are clearly evident in our survey results. Indeed, the storm experiences and negative consequences are described by our survey respondents in powerful and compelling terms.

When it comes to the storm experience, a majority of respondents evacuated, and most were separated from family members over the course of the evacuation and ensuing diaspora. Indeed, the vast majority of evacuees had to move from their homes and seek temporary shelter with relatives or in housing provided by federal, state, and local authorities. In many instances, these temporary accommodations were followed by permanent relocations. Almost one out of three evacuees never returned home, and, simply put, a shocking proportion of survivors were dispersed to unfamiliar and undesirable locations without knowledge of what had happened to loved ones and neighbors. These patterns of residential dislocation occurred for significant numbers of respondents and lasted for extended periods of time. Those who were compelled to relocate to FEMA trailers faced additional health risks due to contamination of the trailers with toxic materials. Many evacuees had to live for six months to more than a year in these dangerous housing alternatives. As with many of our findings, such outcomes were more common for African Americans, prompting additional concerns about racial discrimination and environmental justice.

As survivors faced the arduous task of beginning to rebuild, many unanticipated roadblocks emerged from insurance claims and state grant programs. Although homeowners' insurance claims were generally processed in a timely fashion, there were serious questions about the fairness of the process, with a majority of our respondents reporting significant amounts of stress as they attempted to file claims and obtain due compensation. In addition, the complexities involved in assigning liability and the difficulty in completing the necessary paperwork caused many homeowners to develop adversarial relationships with their insurance carriers. Likewise, though the National Flood Insurance Program processed claims efficiently, not everyone had access to the program, and for many of those who did, the associated bureaucratic red tape was a major impediment to resolving their claims.

Even worse for survivors were the problems and stress associated with the state grant programs created with $20 billion in emergency relief provided by the US Congress. Both the Mississippi Development Authority Homeowner Assistance Program and the Louisiana Road Home Program were characterized by complex and tedious eligibility requirements. In the minds of many, the obstacles associated with insurance claims and state assistance programs constituted a secondary disaster for survivors, as their financial problems were worsened and prolonged.

Our surveys also reveal a serious decline in the physical health of survivors. The exposure to mold, hazardous materials, and deteriorating air quality due to toxic sludge and the burning of debris created very hazardous living conditions. From storm-related oil spills to undetected contamination of toxic chemicals in the air, water, and soil, many survivors of Katrina felt trapped in a prison of poison.[2]

In addition to the incredibly dangerous environment, the lack of health care resources generated numerous medical problems for survivors. This tragic situation is manifested in respondents' perceptions that their health status had declined after the storm, with this trend being more pronounced for African Americans. Specifically, increased headaches, respiratory disorders, hypertension, and heart problems were reported, as well as greater incidence and severity of these symptoms for those who had suffered from such medical conditions prior to the storm. While respiratory problems did decline from 2008 to 2010, high blood pressure and persistent headaches seemed to be lasting health effects of the storm. Furthermore, the anxiety associated with these physical health problems and the potential for toxic contamination exacerbated the mental health consequences of Katrina.

Given the abundant sources of stress for survivors, from health concerns to home destruction to dealing with grant programs, our research on mental and behavioral effects focused on personal depression and post-traumatic stress disorder (PTSD). Findings reveal that one out of every four respondents were at high risk for clinical depression and the majority of our respondents experienced clinical symptoms of PTSD. In the population at large, such patterns of mental disorders are highly correlated with behavioral problems, including substance abuse, domestic violence, and suicide. Once again, these effects were found to be more acute for African Americans. These patterns continued over time; five years after Katrina, serious mental health issues persisted for many survivors in Mississippi and Louisiana.

IMPLICATIONS OF LESSONS LEARNED

Recent developments in climate science suggest that there are likely to be more numerous and more powerful hurricanes in our future.[3] While perhaps not conclusive, hurricanes in 2017 (Harvey, Irma, Maria) and 2018 (Florence, Michael), surely attest to the validity of this projection. At the same time, our basic infrastructure of roads, bridges, levees, storm drains, and sewer and water systems is known to be deteriorating and is growing increasingly vulnerable to storm damage.[4] Based upon these realities, there is little doubt that another Katrina is "coming soon." Thus, we believe it is critical that lessons learned from the Hurricane Katrina experience be more fully elaborated and widely disseminated.

In keeping with this perspective, we now turn to the task of identifying changes in disaster preparedness and emergency management that would mitigate the impact of future storms. Our perspectives come not just from the results of our surveys as reported here, but from an extensive review of disaster-related literature, our own previous academic research, myriad media reports issued before, during, and after major hurricanes, as well as both formal and informal feedback from hurricane survivors, emergency management officials, and community leaders and activists. While there are numerous changes that might have positive impacts, we focus on four areas that appear most relevant and most critical based upon recent experiences.

First, there should be greater emphasis on community involvement in promoting disaster preparedness, as well as in planning for disaster response and recovery. Broader community involvement would not only enhance common knowledge of disaster-related issues and encourage practical preparedness, but also allow for better accommodation of community needs and promote trusting relationships among community members and between community members and emergency management officials.

In academic parlance, these trusting relationships constitute "social capital," which has been shown repeatedly to enhance community resilience,[5] mitigate negative physical health effects[6] and mental health consequences,[7] and facilitate effective disaster response.[8] This is especially important when it comes to issues of race and environmental justice.[9]

To ensure participation of the community at large in activities such as planning meetings and workshops, these efforts should provide meaningful incentives, such as meals, gift cards, or door prizes. This type of community involvement also helps to establish effective lines of communication between citizens and disaster response officials, so critical in times of crisis. These lines of communication could be facilitated and maintained through the creative use of social media to generate hierarchical networks of emergency managers, community leaders, activists, and community members at large.

Community buy-in is particularly important when it comes to facilitating the formulation and implementation of policies necessary to mitigate the impact of hurricanes by updating flood maps, establishing and enforcing elevation requirements for building in hurricane-prone areas, and moving residents from the most vulnerable coastal locations. We believe a comprehensive review designed to guide rethinking and revision of such policies is long overdue. In some cases, for example, coastal homes have been destroyed and rebuilt, only to be destroyed and rebuilt again and again, storm after storm. Programs to move residents from such vulnerable areas are extremely disruptive and have been met with stiff resistance. Broader community understanding and cooperation can be facilitated by greater community involvement in disaster mitigation and emergency management.

A second area where major changes are needed is directly related to the human effects of hurricanes. In disaster recovery, the health of survivors must be a priority. For many vulnerable populations, access to basic primary care is limited by a shortage of providers and the lack of health insurance. When it comes to mental and behavioral health, the situation is even worse; resources for diagnosis and treatment are often extremely limited or nonexistent. Efforts to address these shortcomings must include increased access to care for disadvantaged and underserved communities. This could be accomplished by expanding and further subsidizing the network of Federally Qualified Health Centers that serve poor communities. It might also include adjustments to the Affordable Care Act, expansion of Medicaid, or some entirely new and innovative approach. Increased access is especially critical in addressing mental and behavioral health issues associated with the trauma of the disaster experience. Recent efforts to integrate mental health services into primary care facilities constitute a good start[10] and should be further encouraged and facilitated.

An example of an innovative approach to enhance health care capacity in underserved communities involves using lay health workers to supplement the work of health care professionals and provide a link between the health care system and community members. A pilot project for this approach was instituted under the auspices of the Gulf Region Health Outreach Program after the Deepwater Horizon oil spill.[11] Based upon the principle that a healthy community is a more resilient community, community health workers were trained and placed in a variety of health clinics and community-based organizations in areas affected by the spill. Their activities included promoting disaster preparedness, conducting educational outreach to encourage healthy lifestyles and improve health literacy, and providing referrals and resource guidance as needed, all of which can contribute significantly to improving overall community health.[12]

Alleviating the financial hardships resulting from disasters like Katrina is a third area where changes are needed. When providing funds for disaster relief, Congress should be much more mindful of the obstacles posed by extensive red tape and overly stringent eligibility requirements. It is particularly important to recognize that individuals whose homes have been washed away by a twenty-foot storm surge may not have extensive documentation at hand when asked to produce records and paperwork regarding their needs and losses. In our survey, we found that critically needed disaster relief efforts can add insult to injury if they create inflexible and unresponsive bureaucracies to administer such funding. While we recognize that some may disagree, from our perspective it is better to err on the side of liberality, ensuring that the desperate needs of survivors are met, even if it means that some fraudulent applicants obtain benefits they do not deserve.

A fourth and final suggestion concerns leadership of the American emergency management system. To ensure public engagement in effective emergency preparedness and disaster recovery activities, it is critical that people trust their government.[13] On September 2, 2005, three days after the storm, as conditions throughout the affected area continued to deteriorate into disarray and chaos, President George W. Bush praised the director of the Federal Emergency Management Agency with the infamous quote, "Brownie, you're doing a heck of a job." There was general consensus then as now that Michael Brown was most definitely NOT doing a "heck of a job," but was in fact performing extremely poorly. This should not have been surprising given that Brown was an ineffectual political appointee with vir-

FIGURE 7.4. Department of Homeland Security secretary Michael Chertoff (right) and FEMA director Michael Brown (center) meet with New Orleans mayor Ray Nagin on September 2, 2005. Ten days later, Brown was forced to resign due to incompetence in handling the Katrina disaster. FEMA, photo by Jocelyn Augustino.

tually no experience in emergency management. Stated simply, the most obvious lesson here is that emergency management leadership positions should be staffed on the basis of merit rather than questionable and potentially counterproductive political considerations.

CONCLUSION

Early in the morning hours of August 28, 2005, Hurricane Katrina reached a minimum central pressure of 902 millibars and intensified to a monster Category 5 hurricane with maximum sustained winds of 175 miles per hour. The one silver lining in the dark cloud of Katrina is that hurricanes are unable to maintain this level of ferocity for an extended period of time. To wreak maximum devastation, Katrina would have had to peak a day later. As it happened, by the time the storm made landfall at Buras, Louisiana, at 5:10 a.m. on Monday, August 29, minimum central pressure had increased to 920 millibars and maximum sustained winds had decreased to 127 mph. Given the shocking amount of death, destruction, and disruption wreaked by the storm, it is virtually impossible to imagine what would have happened if Katrina had come ashore at peak strength. With the clear possibility, perhaps probability, of such a large and powerful hurricane making landfall in the United States in the near future, the lessons of Hurricane Katrina should serve as a practical guide in efforts to maximize disaster preparedness, mitigate storm damage, and minimize the trauma of recovery.

THE SAFFIR-SIMPSON
HURRICANE WIND SCALE

The Saffir-Simpson Hurricane Wind Scale is a 1 to 5 categorization based on the hurricane's intensity at the indicated time. The scale—originally developed by wind engineer Herb Saffir and meteorologist Bob Simpson—has been an excellent tool for alerting the public about the possible impacts of various intensity hurricanes. The scale provides examples of the type of damage and impacts in the United States associated with winds of the indicated intensity. In general, damage rises by about a factor of four for every category increase. The maximum sustained surface wind speed (peak one-minute wind at the standard meteorological observation height of ten meters [thirty-three feet] over unobstructed exposure) associated with the cyclone is the determining factor in the scale.

CATEGORY 1
74–95 MPH, 64–82 KNOTS, 119–153 KM/H

Very dangerous winds will produce some damage: Well-constructed frame homes could have damage to roof, shingles, vinyl siding and gutters. Large branches of trees will snap and shallowly rooted trees may be toppled. Extensive damage to power lines and poles likely will result in power outages that could last a few to several days.

CATEGORY 2
96–110 MPH, 83–95 KNOTS, 154–177 KM/H

Extremely dangerous winds will cause extensive damage: Well-constructed frame homes could sustain major roof and siding damage. Many shallowly rooted trees will be snapped or uprooted and block numerous roads. Near-total power loss is expected with outages that could last from several days to weeks.

CATEGORY 3 (MAJOR)
111–129 MPH, 96–112 KNOTS, 178–208 KM/H

Devastating damage will occur: Well-built framed homes may incur major damage or removal of roof decking and gable ends. Many trees will be snapped or uprooted, blocking numerous roads. Electricity and water will be unavailable for several days to weeks after the storm passes.

CATEGORY 4 (MAJOR)
130–156 MPH, 113–136 KNOTS, 209–251 KM/H

Catastrophic damage will occur: Well-built framed homes can sustain severe damage with loss of most of the roof structure and/or some exterior walls. Most trees will be snapped or uprooted and power poles downed. Fallen trees and power poles will isolate residential areas. Power outages will last weeks to possibly months. Most of the area will be uninhabitable for weeks or months.

CATEGORY 5 (MAJOR)
157 MPH OR HIGHER, 137 KNOTS OR HIGHER, 252 KM/H OR HIGHER

Catastrophic damage will occur: A high percentage of framed homes will be destroyed, with total roof failure and wall collapse. Fallen trees and power poles will isolate residential areas. Power outages will last for weeks to possibly months. Most of the area will be uninhabitable for weeks or months.

Adapted from "Saffir-Simpson Hurricane Wind Scale," National Hurricane Center, https://www.nhc.noaa.gov/aboutsshws.php.

SURVEY METHODOLOGY

HURRICANE KATRINA SURVIVOR SURVEYS
2008 SURVEY

Instrument: A survey instrument of 120 items was developed using a variety of measures and scales. It included 110 questions about actual storm experiences, evacuation behaviors, property damage and economic loss, psychological and physical health consequences, status of recovery, and expectation for the future. It also included ten questions regarding the respondents' demographic characteristics of age, sex, race, marital status, education, pre-Katrina employment, current work status and occupation, and number of children in household. The instrument was extensively reviewed, pretested, and revised where appropriate.

Sample: The target population included all adult residents (over age eighteen) of two counties in Mississippi (Hancock and Harrison) and five parishes in Louisiana (Jefferson, Orleans, Plaquemines, St. Bernard, and St. Tammany). For Mississippi, an appropriate sampling frame of thirty thousand geographically targeted random-digit dialed telephone numbers was purchased from ASDE Survey Sampler. Experience with the Mississippi sample suggested that this sample was significantly larger than needed, so for Louisiana a sample of fifteen thousand telephone numbers was purchased. Within each household, participation of adult respondents was randomized using "most recent birthday" criteria ("May I speak to the person in your household who is eighteen or older and has had the most recent birthday").

Interviewing: The interviews were conducted by the USA Polling Group, a multidisciplinary survey research center located on the University of South Alabama's main campus in Mobile, Alabama. Over its nine-year history, the Polling Group has conducted over 550 surveys using a state-of-the-art computer-assisted telephone interview system.

In randomizing within households, if the correct person was not available, an appointment was made to call back. Each telephone number was eligible for up to seven call-backs unless there was a firm refusal. In Mississippi, 810 interviews were completed between April 16 and May 28, 2008, and in Louisiana, 1,738 interviews were completed between June 2 and August 27, 2008, yielding a grand total of 2,548 completed interviews. Interviews took an average of 17.25 minutes to complete. Part of the interviewing processes included gathering contact information from respondents to build a panel for future interviews; a total of 1,458 respondents provided such information for the 2010 Survey.

Results of telephone contacts were as follows:

	Mississippi	Louisiana
Refusals	1,007	5,519
Language, hearing, illness	51	155
Pending appointments	118	148
Incomplete interviews	36	78
Completed interviews	810	1,738
Total household contacts	2,022	7,638
Interview participation rate	40%	23%
Provided panel information	453	905
Panel participation	56%	52%

The participation rate is calculated by dividing completed interviews by total household contacts. One could make the case for subtracting pending appointments and language, hearing, and illness problems from total household contacts before the calculation since these are not refusals; this approach would result in participation rates of 44 percent in Mississippi and 24 percent in Louisiana.

Sampling Error: With a total of 2,548 interviews completed, the margin of error for the full sample is +/– 1.9 percent at the 95 percent confidence level. This means we are 95 percent sure that the results for any given item obtained in the survey are within 1.9 percent of the results that would have been obtained if the entire adult population of the target area had been surveyed. Sampling error for the 810 Mississippi interviews is +/– 3.4 percent at the 95 percent confidence level. Sampling error for the 1,738 Louisiana interviews is +/– 2.4 percent at the 95 percent confidence level. Sample error for subgroup comparisons will vary based upon the size of the subgroup.

2010 SURVEY

Instrument: The survey instrument was a scaled-down version of the 2008 instrument. It included sixty questions about hurricane experiences and status of recovery, plus seven demographic questions.

Sample: The sample consisted of contact data provided by the USA Polling Group, which included a total of 1,352 valid names with complete contact information.

Interviewing: Interviews were conducted by the University of North Florida Polling Lab. A total of 466 interviews were completed. This represents a response rate of about 35 percent. Each number was eligible for up to seven call-backs unless there was a firm refusal. Overall, approximately 53,500 calls were made during the data collection period.

A review of the dispositions indicates that the primary reason for failing to contact respondents was that the phone number was no longer valid. Of the 2008 respondents who were contacted in 2010, only approximately 10 percent refused to participate in the survey.

Sampling Error: With a sample of 466, sampling error is +/−4.5 percent at the 95 percent confidence level. Sample error for subgroup comparisons will vary based upon the size of the subgroup.

NOTES

CHAPTER 1. INTRODUCTION

1. While a much larger area was affected by Katrina, various constraints necessitate limits on the size and jurisdictional boundaries of the target area for our study. Based upon the severity and geographical extent of the damage, we identified Hancock and Harrison Counties in Mississippi and Orleans, Jefferson, St. Bernard, Plaquemines, and St. Tammany Parishes in Louisiana as constituting the most appropriate and feasible target area.

2. The Saffir-Simpson Hurricane Wind Scale is designed to help determine wind hazards of an approaching hurricane. For a full description of the scale, see appendix 1.

3. For detailed information on survey methodology and sampling error, see appendix 2.

4. The deadliest storm to strike the United States in modern times was the Great Galveston Hurricane of 1900, for which estimates of fatalities range from six thousand to twelve thousand.

5. EBSCO is a leading resource for identifying and accessing scholarly research across a full range of subject matter, whether generated by academic institutions, governmental agencies, or private research organizations.

6. Narayan Sastry, "Tracing the Effects of Hurricane Katrina on the Population of New Orleans: The Displaced New Orleans Residents Pilot Study," *Sociological Methods and Research* 38, no. 1 (2009): 171–196.

7. Thompson E. Davis III, Amie E. Grills-Taquechel, and Thomas H. Ollendick, "The Psychological Impact from Hurricane Katrina: Effects of Displacement and Trauma Exposure on University Students," *Behavior Therapy* 41, no. 3 (2010): 340–349.

8. Lynda C. Burton, Elizabeth A. Skinner, Lori Uscher-Pines, Richard Lieberman, Bruce Leff, Rebecca Clark, Qilu Yu et al., "Health of Medicare Advantage Plan Enrollees at One Year after Hurricane Katrina," *American Journal of Managed Care* 15, no. 1 (2009): 13–22.

9. Ronald C. Kessler, Sandro Galea, Russell T. Jones, and Holly A. Parker, "Mental Illness and Suicidality after Hurricane Katrina," *Bulletin of the World Health Organization* 84, no. 12 (2006): 930–939.

10. Neil Malhotra and Alexander G. Kuo, "Emotions as Moderators of Information Cue Use: Citizen Attitudes toward Hurricane Katrina," *American Politics Research* 37, no. 2 (2009): 301–326; Keith Nicholls and J. Steven Picou, "The Impact of Hurricane Katrina on Trust in Government," *Social Science Quarterly* 94, no. 2 (2013): 344–361.

11. Julia A. Flagg, "The Social Consequences of a Natural/Technological Disaster: Evidence from Louisiana and Mississippi," *Local Environment* 22, no. 3 (2017): 306–320.

12. As a result of climate change, it is doubtful that Hurricane Katrina will maintain this distinction throughout the remainder of the twenty-first century; nevertheless, we maintain that the label is valid as of this writing. Even the trauma of Hurricanes Maria or Harvey in 2017 or Florence in 2018 pale in comparison with the nightmare of Katrina.

CHAPTER 2. EXPERIENCING KATRINA

1. "Hurricane Katrina Updates on NOLA.com," *New Orleans Times-Picayune*, August 29, 2005, accessed January 15, 2019, http://www.nola.com/katrina/index .ssf/2005/08/online_times-picayune_news_blo.html.

2. "Environmental Public Health Impacts of Disasters: Hurricane Katrina: Workshop Summary," chapter 3, *Hurricane Katrina: Challenges for the Community* (Washington, DC: National Academies Press, 2007), accessed January 15, 2019, https://www.nap.edu/read/11840/chapter/5.

3. National Center for Missing and Exploited Children, *Final Report: Katrina/ Rita Missing Persons Hotline Update on Calls/Cases, Wednesday 3/22/2006*, http:// www.missingkids.com/home/site-search?search=katrina.

4. Anne Mercuri and Holly L. Angelique, "Children's Responses to Natural, Technological, and Na-Tech Disasters," *Community Mental Health Journal* 40, no. 2 (April 2004): 167–175.

5. J. Steven Picou and Brent K. Marshall, "Social Impacts of Hurricane Katrina on Displaced K-12 Students and Educational Institutions in Coastal Alabama Counties: Some Preliminary Observations," *Sociological Spectrum* 27, no. 6 (2007): 767–780.

6. "New Orleans Will Force Evacuations; Superdome, Refuge for Thousands, May Be Torn Down," CNN, September 7, 2005, accessed January 16, 2019, http:// www.cnn.com/2005/US/09/06/katrina.impact/.

7. Danny D. Reible, Charles N. Haas, John H. Pardue, and William J. Walsh, "Toxic and Contaminant Concerns Generated by Hurricane Katrina," *Journal of Environmental Engineering* 132, no. 6 (2006): 565–566.

CHAPTER 3. THE LONG ROAD HOME

1. From the 2000 census to one year after the storm, the population of New Orleans had dropped by about 250,000. Although the population has since rebounded, much of the increase is from new residents rather than returnees. Furthermore, based on 2015 projections, the population is still only 80 percent of what it

was before the storm. See Alyson Plyer, "Facts for Features: The Katrina Impact," *The Data Center*, accessed January 18, 2019, https://www.datacenterresearch.org /data-resources/katrina/facts-for-impact/.

2. Jeffrey A. Groen and Anne E. Polivka, "Going Home after Hurricane Katrina: Determinants of Return Migration and Changes in Affected Areas," Working Paper 48, US Bureau of Labor Statistics, September 2009.

3. Richard Morin and Lisa Rein, "Some of the Uprooted Won't Go Home Again," *Washington Post*, September 16, 2005, accessed February 3, 2019, http://www .washingtonpost.com/wp-dyn/content/article/2005/09/15/AR2005091502010.html.

4. David W. Moore, "At Least 100,000 Katrina Victims Still Separated from Families: Half of Victims Who Requested Red Cross Aid Still Living in Temporary Housing or Shelter," Gallup News Service, October 14, 2005; accessed January 19, 2019, https://news.gallup.com/poll/19225/least-100000-katrina-victims-still-sepa rated-from-families.aspx.

5. "Hurricane Katrina," Louisiana Society for the Prevention of Cruelty to Animals, accessed January 19, 2019, https://www.la-spca.org/katrina.

6. Federal Emergency Management Agency, "Frequently Requested National Statistics Hurricane Katrina—One Year Later Fact Sheet," http://www.fema.gov /hazard/hurricane/2005katrina/anniversary_factsheet.shtm.

7. Center for Disease Control and Prevention, "Fact Sheet: Final Report on Formaldehyde Levels in FEMA-Supplied Travel Trailers, Park Models, and Mobile Homes," July 2, 2008, Amended December 15, 2010, https://www.cdc.gov/asthma /community-health/trailerstudy/default.htm.

CHAPTER 4. EMERGING OBSTACLES TO REBUILDING

1. "Hurricane Katrina: Rebuilding the Gulf Coast Region," George W. Bush White House Archives, accessed January 20, 2019, https://georgewbush-whitehouse .archives.gov/infocus/katrina/.

2. "Disaster Oversight: Hurricane Katrina," Department of Housing and Urban Development, accessed February 3, 2019, https://www.hudoig.gov/disaster_oversight /krw.

3. Details of the Mississippi program were obtained on the Mississippi Development Authority's website, http://www.mississippi.org/assets/docs/community /ms2008ai_final.pdf?zoom_highlight=katrina#search="katrina."

4. Details of the Louisiana Program were obtained from Road Home Program website, https://www.road2la.org/HAP/Default.aspx, and the Rebuilding Louisiana website, http://www.rebuild.la.gov/.

CHAPTER 5. PHYSICAL HEALTH EFFECTS

1. J. Steven Picou and Brent K. Marshall, "Katrina as Paradigm-Shift: Reflections on Disaster Research in the Twenty-First Century," in *The Sociology of Katrina: Perspectives on a Modern Catastrophe*, 1st ed., edited by David L. Brunsma, David Overfelt, and J. Steven Picou (Lanham, MD: Rowman and Littlefield, 2007), 1–20.

2. "Katrina in Perspective," chap. 1 in *The Federal Response to Hurricane Katrina: Lessons Learned*, George W. Bush White House Archives, accessed January 21, 2019, https://georgewbush-whitehouse.archives.gov/reports/katrina-lessons-learned/chapter1.html.

3. Robert Esworthy, Linda-Jo Schierow, Claudia Copeland, Linda Luther, and Jonathan L. Ramseur, "Cleanup after Hurricane Katrina: Environmental Considerations," Resources, Science, and Industry Division, Congressional Research Service, Library of Congress, May 3, 2006, accessed January 21, 2019, http://congressional research.com/RL33115/document.php?study=Cleanup+after+Hurricane+Katrina+Environmental+Considerations.

4. "Hurricane Katrina: Continuing Debris Removal and Disposal Issues," US Government Accountability Office, August 25, 2008, accessed January 21, 2019, https://www.gao.gov/assets/100/95709.html.

5. "Katrina by the Numbers: Need for Health Care Assistance in Louisiana," Center for American Progress, October 7, 2005, accessed January 21, 2019, https://www.americanprogress.org/issues/healthcare/news/2005/10/07/1698/katrina-by-the-numbers-need-for-health-care-assistance-in-louisiana/.

6. *Hurricane Katrina in the Gulf Coast: Mitigation Assessment Team Report, Building Performance Observations, Recommendations, and Technical Guidance*, section 8-4-2, "Overview of Hurricane Katrina in the New Orleans Area," FEMA Report 549, July 2006, accessed January 21, 2019, https://www.fema.gov/media-library/assets/documents/4069?id=1857.

CHAPTER 6. MENTAL HEALTH EFFECTS

1. "Assessment of Health-Related Needs after Hurricanes Katrina and Rita, Orleans and Jefferson Parishes, New Orleans Area, Louisiana, October 17–22, 2005," Morbidity and Mortality Weekly Report, Centers for Disease Control and Prevention, January 20, 2006, accessed January 22, 2019, https://www.cdc.gov/mmwr/preview/mmwrhtml/mm5502a5.htm.

2. Philip S. Wang, Michael J. Gruber, Richard E. Powers, Michael Schoenbaum, Anthony H. Speier, Kenneth B. Wells, and Ronald C. Kessler, "Mental Health Service Use among Hurricane Katrina Survivors in the Eight Months after the Disaster," *Psychiatric Services* 58, no. 11 (2007): 1403–1411.

3. Mordecai N. Potash and Daniel K. Winstead, "A Review of Mental Health

Issues as a Result of Hurricane Katrina," *Psychiatric Annals* 38, no. 2 (2008), DOI: 10.3928/00485713-20080201-08.

4. Gary Sheets, "Mental Patients Have Nowhere to Go," *New Orleans Times-Picayune*, April 23, 2007, accessed January 22, 2019, http://blog.nola.com/topnews /2007/04/mental_patients_have_nowhere_t.html.

5. It is simply not feasible to ask the full universe of potentially interesting and relevant questions in a telephone survey. In order to maximize participation and minimize incomplete surveys, we limited our survey instrument to 123 questions.

6. For a relatively comprehensive review, see Gemma Vilagut, Carlos G. Forero, Gabriela Barbaglia, and Jordi Alonso, "Screening for Depression in the General Population with the Center for Epidemiologic Studies Depression (CES-D): A Systematic Review with Meta-Analysis," *Plos ONE* 11, no. 5 (2016): e0155431, accessed January 24, 2019, https://doi.org/10.1371/journal.pone.0155431.

7. Lenore Sawyer Radloff, "The CES-D Scale: A Self-Report Depression Scale for Research in the General Population," *Applied Psychological Measurement* 1, no. 3 (1977): 385–401.

8. Eva C. Sundin and Mardi J. Horowitz, "Horowitz's Impact of Event Scale Evaluation of Twenty Years of Use," *Psychosomatic Medicine* 65, no. 5 (2003): 870–876.

9. Daniel S. Weiss and Charles R. Marmar, "The Impact of Event Scale— Revised," in *Assessing Psychological Trauma and PTSD*, edited by John P. Wilson and Terence M. Keene (New York: Guilford Press, 1996), 399–411.

10. Since differences in the amount of missing data in the two surveys would tend to muddle these comparisons, we exclude missing data, reporting results only for those who answered the questions.

CHAPTER 7. SUMMING UP AND LESSONS LEARNED

1. J. Steven Picou, "Katrina as a Natech Disaster: Toxic Contamination and Long-Term Risks for Residents of New Orleans," *Journal of Applied Social Science* 3, no. 2 (2009): 39–55.

2. Ibid.

3. For a well-documented and comprehensive discussion of the impact of climate change on hurricane activity, see "Global Warming and Hurricanes: An Overview of Current Research Results," Geophysical Fluid Dynamics Laboratory, National Oceanic and Atmospheric Administration, accessed January 26, 2019, https://www.gfdl.noaa.gov/global-warming-and-hurricanes/#early-gfdl-research -on-global-warming-and-hurricanes.

4. For example, the American Society of Civil Engineers gives US infrastructure a grade of D+. See "2017 Infrastructure Report Card," accessed January 26, 2019, https://www.infrastructurereportcard.org/.

5. Betty Pfefferbaum, Richard L. Van Horn, and Rose L. Pfefferbaum, "A Con-

ceptual Framework to Enhance Community Resilience Using Social Capital," *Clinical Social Work Journal* 45, no. 2 (2017): 102–110; Daniel P. Aldrich and Michelle A. Meyer, "Social Capital and Community Resilience," *American Behavioral Scientist* 59, no. 2 (2015): 254–269.

6. Francis O. Adeola and J. Steven Picou, "Race, Social Capital, and the Health Impacts of Katrina: Evidence from the Louisiana and Mississippi Gulf Coast," *Human Ecology Review* 19, no. 1 (2012): 10–24.

7. Francis O. Adeola and J. Steven Picou, "Social Capital and the Mental Health Impacts of Hurricane Katrina: Assessing Long-Term Patterns of Psychosocial Distress," *International Journal of Mass Emergencies and Disasters* 32, no. 1 (2014): 121–156.

8. Fran H. Norris, Susan P. Stevens, Betty Pfefferbaum, Karen F. Wyche, and Rose L. Pfefferbaum, "Community Resilience as a Metaphor, Theory, Set of Capacities, and Strategy for Disaster Readiness," *American Journal of Community Psychology* 41, no. 1–2 (2008): 127–150.

9. Francis O. Adeola and J. Steven Picou, "Hurricane Katrina-linked Environmental Injustice: Race, Class, and Place Differentials in Attitudes," *Disasters* 41, no. 2 (2017): 228–257.

10. Anna Durbin, Janet Durbin, Jennifer M. Hensel, and Raisa Deber, "Barriers and Enablers to Integrating Mental Health into Primary Care: A Policy Analysis," *Journal of Behavioral Health Services and Research* 43, no. 1 (2016): 127–139; for a helpful discussion of integrated care, see "Integrated Care," National Institute of Mental Health, accessed January 27, 2019, https://www.nimh.nih.gov/health/topics/integrated-care/index.shtml.

11. This portion of the Gulf Region Health Outreach Program was implemented by the Coastal Resource and Resiliency Center at the University of South Alabama. The Gulf Region Health Outreach Program was funded from the Deepwater Horizon medical benefits class action settlement, which was approved by the US district court in New Orleans on January 11, 2013.

12. Keith Nicholls, J. Steven Picou, Joycelyn Curtis, and Janel A. Lowman, "The Utility of Community Health Workers in Disaster Preparedness, Recovery, and Resiliency," *Journal of Applied Social Science* 9, no. 2 (2015): 191–202.

13. Keith Nicholls and J. Steven Picou, "The Impact of Hurricane Katrina on Trust in Government," *Social Science Quarterly* 94, no. 2 (2013): 344–361.

INDEX

Note: Page numbers in *italics* indicate tables, charts, and photographs.

deaths from Katrina. *See* casualty estimates

debris from storm, 31, *31*, 46, *59*, 59–60, 63–64, 76, 89, 91

decisions to return, 30–37, 76

deductibles, 46–47

Deepwater Horizon oil spill, 94

dehydration, 64

demographics of study, 5–6, *7*, 99, 100–101

demolition process, *44*

Department of Homeland Security, *95*

Department of Housing and Urban Development, 51–52

depopulation of region, 34, 103n1

depression: immediate injuries contrasted with, 74; incidence of, *78*, *80*; and ongoing effects of Katrina, 86, 91–92; racial disparities in rates of, *82*; rates over time, *83*; and scope and organization of study, 8; survey measurements of, 77–79; symptoms of, *78*, *79*

diagnosis of health problems, 71

disaster preparedness, 92–95

disaster relief funds, 94

diseases, 64

displacements, 25–28; breakdown of post-storm, *32*; and decision to return, 30–37; effects of long-term, 27, 36–37; length of, 32–37, *33*, *35*; and mental health effects of Katrina, *75*, *81*; and number of evacuees, 2; and ongoing effects of Katrina, 86–87; and scope and organization of study, 8

divorces, 72

documenting effects of Katina, 89–90

domestic violence, 80

drowning deaths, 28, *59*, 63

Dust Bowl, 25

EBSCO, 10, 102n5

economic effects of Katrina, 23–25; and context of study, 9, 10; and decisions to return, 34; and mental health effects, *75*, *81*; and summary of study findings, *90*, 94

education of respondents, *7*

electricity failures, 64

electrocution risk, 8

electronic equipment waste, 63

emergency management practices, 92–95

employment status of respondents, *7*, 76

environmental conditions, 60–65. *See also* hazardous materials exposure

Environmental Protection Agency (EPA), 28

evacuations: and complications for evacuees, 14; difficulties of, 11, 16; and family separations, 8; and geographic locations of evacuees, 16–17, 27; prior to landfall, 25; mandatory, 13–14, 16, 26; and mental health effects of Katrina, 75–76; and number of evacuees, 2; and ongoing effects of Katrina, 90; personal accounts of, 1; and survey responses, 16, *16*; trauma associated with, 20; voluntary, 14. *See also* displacements; rescues

family separations: and accounts of respondents, 17–20; and Astrodome reunification center, *18*; length of, *37*; and mental health effects of Katrina, *75*, *81*; and ongoing effects of Katrina, 90; and recovery phase, 30; and reunifications, 37–38; and scope and organization of study, 8; by state, *19*; stress and anxiety of, 18

Federal Emergency Management Agency (FEMA), *15*, 94. *See also* FEMA trailers

Federally Qualified Health Centers, 93

FEMA trailers, 29, 36–37, 39–42, *40*, 70, 75

financial effects of Katrina. *See* economic effects of Katrina

flashbacks, 72

flooding and flood damage: areas prone to, 21; incidence of, *22*; and levee failures, 2, 5, 20, 59–61, 64, 92; and New Orleans canals, 5; post-storm, 8, 22, 30–31, 45–46; and post-storm displacements, 27; in residential areas, *49*; and scope of Katrina damage, 22. *See also* flood insurance flood insurance: claims and settlement process, 48–51; and homeowners' insurance, 45–48; and Louisiana Road Home Program, 54–55; and Mississippi Development Authority, 53; and National Flood Insurance Program (NFIP), 43, 45, 48–49, 53, 91; and primary sources of recovery funds, 43–45; and the Road Home Program, 43; and scope of study, 11; and status of claims by state, *50*; stress associated with, *51*, 56, *56*, *75*, 91

Florida, 3

follow-up surveys, 87–88

food shortages, 64

formaldehyde exposure, 39, 41, 70

French Quarter, 26

Freon leaks, 63

frequency of hurricanes, 9, 34–35, 92

Gallup polls, 38

Galveston Hurricane of 1900, 102n4

gas shortages, 18

grant programs: described, 51–52; Louisiana Road Home Program, 54–55; Mississippi Homeowner Assistance Program, 52–54; and ongoing effects of Katrina, 90–91; as primary sources of recovery funds, 43–45, *44*; stress and anxiety associated with, 56–57, *75*

Great Galveston Hurricane of 1900, 102n4

Gulf of Mexico, 3, 61–63, 88

Gulf Region Health Outreach Program, 94

Hancock County, Mississippi, 4, 33, 53, 99

Harrison County, Mississippi, 33, 53, 99

hazardous materials exposure: and debris from storm, *59*; and environmental conditions after Katrina, 60–65; and FEMA trailers, 39–42, 70; and mental health effects of Katrina, *75*, *81*; and "nonpoint pollution," 63; personal accounts of, 58; and post-disaster dangers of Katrina, 8; and scope of study, 11; study findings on, 91; survey mea-

surements of, 28, 68–70, *69*; testing for, *62*

headaches, 58, *67*, 71

health care resources, 10, 60, 64–65, 93–94

heart problems, 8, 12, 58, 59, 65–67, *67*, 91

Hispanics, x, 35, *35*

homeowners' insurance, 11, 43, *47*, *56*, 91. *See also* flood insurance

home repair expenses, 23, 24, *24*, *75*

hospital facilities, 64–65. *See also* health care resources

housing: abandoned, 88; affordable, 2, 27; habitability of, 6, 25–27, *27*, 32, 34, 98; and homeowners' insurance, 11, 43, *47*, *56*, 91; and home repair expenses, 23, 24, *24*, *75*; shortages, 2, 64; temporary, 39–42, 90 (*see also* FEMA trailers)

Houston, Texas, 13, *18*, 34, *73*

Hurricane Camille, 13

Hurricane Cindy, 35

Hurricane Dennis, 35

Hurricane Florence, 92, 103n12

Hurricane Harvey, 92, 103n12

Hurricane Irma, 92

Hurricane Ivan, 34–35

Hurricane Katrina Homeowner Assistance Grant Program, 43–45, 52, 91

Hurricane Maria, 92, 103n12

Hurricane Michael, 92

Hurricane Rita, 35

hypertension, 12, 58, 65–67, *67*, 71, 91

Impact of Events Scale, 77, *80*, 85

inability to evacuate, 16

income disparities, 17

industrial facilities, 28

infrastructure damage, 10, 11, 31, *73*, 92

injuries from Katrina, 59. *See also* casualty estimates

insect infestations, 8, 60, 63

insurance claims and settlements: and financial effects of Katrina, 23; and homeowners' insurance, 45–48; and mental health effects of Katrina, *75*; and ongoing effects of Katrina, 90–91; as primary sources of recovery

funds, 43–45, *44*; and scope and organization of study, 6; status of, by state, *47*; stress associated with, 45–48, *48*, 50–51, *51*, *56*, 56–57, *75*, 91
interview procedures, 5–6, 99–101, 106n5, 106n10
Intrusive Recollections measure, 77, 79

Jackson County, Mississippi, 53
Jefferson Parish, 73, 99

Keesler Air Force Base, *44*

Lake Borgne, 4
Lake Ponchartrain, 61–63
landfalls of Katrina, 3, 4, 16
lawsuits, 43, 46–47, *75*
lead contamination, 68
length of displacements, 32–37, *33*, *35*
lessons learned from Katrina, 11, 92–95
levee failures, 2, 5, 20, 59–61, 64, 92
literature review, 10–12
Louisiana: and disparities in financial impact of Katrina, 24–25; and family separations, 18, *19*, *37*, 38; and FEMA trailers, 41; hazardous materials exposures in, 28; and insurance claims, 46, 47, 48, *48*, *50*, 51, *51*; and ongoing effects of Katrina, *88*; and physical health effects of Katrina, 65; and post-storm displacements, 27, 33, *33*; and racial disparities in evacuation patterns, 17; and residential damage, 20, 22; and state grant programs, 52; and survey participation rate, 100
Louisiana Road Home Program, 43–44, 52, 54–55, *55*, *56*, 56–57, 91
Louisiana Society for the Prevention of Cruelty to Animals, 38
lung cancer, 58

mandatory evacuations, 13–14, 16, 26
Medicaid, 93
mental health effects of Katrina: and context of study, 9; and FEMA trailers, 41; and long-term displacements, 36; ongoing, 85, 86, 91–92; post-traumatic

stress disorder (PTSD), 8, 74, 77–81, *81*, *82*, *83*, 85–86, 91–92; racial disparities in, 81–83; scope of, 72–74; and scope and organization of study, 5, 8–9, 12; and sources of stress and trauma, 74–77, *75*; summary of study findings on, *90*; survey measurements of, 77–81, 99. *See also* stress and anxiety
mercury contamination, 68
Metairie, Louisiana, *26*
missing data, 106n10
Mississippi: disparities of financial impact of Katrina in, 24–25; and family separations, 18, *19*, *37*, 38; and FEMA trailers, 41; hazardous materials exposures in, 28; and insurance claims, 46–48, *47*, *48*, *50*, 51, *51*; and Katrina's landfall, 4; and ongoing effects of Katrina, 88, *88*; and physical health effects of Katrina, 65; and post-storm displacements, 27, 33, *33*; and racial disparities in evacuation patterns, 17; and residential damage, 20, 22; and state grant programs, 52; and survey participation rate, 100
Mississippi Development Authority (MDA), 43–44, 52–54, *54*, *56*, 57, 91
Mississippi Sound, 9
mobile homes, 36. *See also* FEMA trailers
mold, 60, *61*, 68, 69, 91
mortgage insurance, 49
Murphy Oil USA Refinery, 61
mycotoxins, 69

Nagin, Ray, 13, 26, 31, *95*
"natech disasters," 60
National Center for Missing and Exploited Children, 18
National Flood Insurance Program (NFIP), 43, 45, 48–49, 53, 91
National Hurricane Center, 3, *4*, 14–16
Native Americans, *35*
nausea/stomach problems, *67*
New Orleans: damage to municipal services in, 34; flood damage in, *49*; infrastructure damage in, 25–26; and

Katrina's approach and evacuation
orders, 13; neighborhoods in, damaged
by Katrina, 8; and path of Katrina,
4, 14; post-storm flooding in, 8; and
Road Home Program, 43; Superdome
evacuees in, *15. See also specific neighborhoods and parishes*
New Orleans East, 5
Ninth Ward, 5, 13
nonpoint pollution, 63

oil spills, 91, 94
ongoing effects of Katrina, 2, 85, 87–89
Orleans Parish, 73, 99

panel for future interviews, 6
Pass Christian, Mississippi, *59*, 89
path of Katrina, 1, 3–4, *4*, 14, 22, 102n1
pathogens, 60. *See also* hazardous materials exposure
Pearl River County, Mississippi, 53
persistence of Katrina effects, 2, 7–8,
85–87, 87–89
personal accounts: of evacuation experiences, *16*; of FEMA trailers, 29; of
Katrina's approach and evacuation
orders, 1, 13; of mental health effects
of Katrina, 72; of ongoing effects of
Katrina, 86; of physical health effects
of Katrina, 58; of Road Home Program, 43
pessimism about Katrina recovery, 86,
87–89, *88*
pest animals, 8, 60, 63
pets, 38, 63
physical damage of Katrina: and context
of study, 9; and debris, 31, *31*, 46, *59*,
59–60, 63–64, 76, 89, 91; extent of, 6;
and home losses, 6; and home repair
expenses, 23, 24, *24*, *75*; and injuries,
58–59 (*see also* casualty estimates);
and length of displacements, 33–36;
and Saffir-Simpson Hurricane Wind
Scale, 97–98; and wind damage, 20,
22, *22*, 45–46. *See also* flooding and
flood damage; hazardous materials
exposure; physical health effects of
Katrina

physical health effects of Katrina: and
changes over time, 70–71; and context
of study, 9; and environmental conditions, 60–65; and FEMA trailers,
39–42, 70; ongoing, 90, *90*; personal
accounts of, 86; racial disparities in,
67; and scope and organization of
study, 8, 10; scope of, 58–60; survey
measurements of, 65–70, *71*
Plaquemines Parish, 99
political influences, 94–95
political leadership, 10
pollution. *See* hazardous materials
exposure
poor communities, 93
Port Sulfur, Louisiana, *21*, *31*
post-storm flooding, 8, 22, 30–31, 45–46
post-traumatic stress disorder (PTSD), 8,
74, 77–81, *81*, *82*, *83*, 85–86, 91–92
preexisting health conditions, 67–68, *68*
profit losses, 23
psychological effects. *See* mental health
effects of Katrina

quality of life, 8–9, 10

racial and ethnic disparities: in evacuation patterns, 16–17; and family separations, 20, 38; and FEMA trailer
problems, 39; and financial effects of
Katrina, 23–25, *24*; and grant program
outcomes, 53–54, 57; and habitability
of homes after storm, *27*; and hazardous materials exposure, 39; and insurance claims, 48, 51; and length of
displacements, 33; and mental health
effects of Katrina, 81–83, *82*; and ongoing effects of Katrina, 90–91; and
physical health effects of Katrina, 66,
66, *67*
racial makeup of study participants, *7*
randomization techniques, 5, 99–100
rapid growth of storm, 1
recovery phase: and community life,
29–30; and decision to return, 30–37;
and family reunifications, 37–38; and
scope of study, 11; and temporary
housing, 39–42, 90

Red Cross, 38, *73*
Renaissance Village, 29
renters, 30
reopening of neighborhoods, 26–27, 31
rescues: of animals and pets, 38; as cause
    of family separations, 18; and deci-
    sions to return, 32; and mental health
    effects of Katrina, 75; personal ac-
    counts of, 13, *16*, 17
research on Katrina effects, 10–12
residential damage, 20–23, *21*, *22*, 75
resiliency of communities, 9–10, 93, 94
respiratory problems, 58, 64, *67*, 69–70,
    91
road damage, 64
Road Home Program. *See* Louisiana Road
    Home Program

Saffir, Herb, 97
Saffir-Simpson Hurricane Wind Scale, 3,
    97–98, 102n2
sampling error rate, 100–101
Sebren, Windi, 86
sewerage systems, 28, 60, 64
sex of respondents, 7
sheltering in place, 12, 14, *16*, 16–17, 18,
    75, 89
Simpson, Bob, 97
Six Flags Amusement Park, 88, *89*
social capital, 93
social damage caused by Katrina, 7–8, 73
social engagement, 92–95
socioeconomic vulnerabilities, 20–21. *See
    also* economic effects of Katrina
sociological damage of Katrina, *90*
state grant programs, 51–52, 56. *See also*
    Louisiana Road Home Program;
    Mississippi Development Authority
    (MDA)
St. Bernard Parish, 5, *62*, 99
storm surge damage, 1, 20–22, *21*, *22*,
    45–46, 64. *See also* flooding and flood
    damage
stress and anxiety: and grant programs,
    52, 53, 55, *56*; and hazardous materials
    exposure, 28; and insurance claims,
    45–48, *48*, 50–51, *51*, 56, *56*, 57, 75, 91;
    and physical health effects of Katrina,

59, 69–70, 70–71; and post-traumatic
    stress disorder (PTSD), 8, 74, 77–81,
    81, *82*, *83*, 85–86, 91–92; and scope and
    organization of study, 8; sources of,
    74–76. *See also* mental health effects
    of Katrina
St. Tammany Parish, 99
substance abuse, 80, 92
suicides, 80, 92
Superdome evacuees, *15*, *84*
Superfund National Priority List sites,
    28, 61
survey research methodology, 5–6,
    99–101

telephone interview procedures, 5–6,
    99–101, 106n5, 106n10
temporary housing, 39–42, 90. *See also*
    FEMA trailers
thallium contamination, 68
Times-Picayune, 73–74
toxic contamination. *See* hazardous
    materials exposure
trauma, 74–76. *See also* post-traumatic
    stress disorder (PTSD)

uninhabitable structures, 6, 25–26, 32, 34,
    98. *See also* displacements
University of North Florida Polling Lab,
    101
Uptown, 26
USA Polling Group, 99, 101
US Congress, 49, 51, 91, 94
US Government Accounting Office, 63
USNS *Comfort*, 65
utility services, 63–64

vehicular debris, 63
voluntary evacuations, 14
vulnerability of communities, 9–10

wage losses, 23
Washington Post, 34
water quality, 60, 64
Waveland, Mississippi, 88
wind damage, 20, 22, *22*, 45–46
wind speeds of Katrina, xi, 1–4, *2*, 13,
    95–97